JACK HIBBS

CALLED TO TAKE A
BOLD
STAND

HARVEST HOUSE PUBLISHERS
EUGENE, OREGON

Unless otherwise indicated, all Scripture verses are taken from the New King James Version®. Copyright © 1982 by Thomas Nelson. Used with permission. All rights reserved.

Verses marked NLT are taken from the *Holy Bible*, New Living Translation, copyright © 1996, 2004, 2015 by Tyndale House Foundation. Used with permission of Tyndale House Publishers, Inc., Carol Stream, Illinois 60188. All rights reserved.

Verses marked KJV are taken from the King James Version of the Bible.

Verses marked NIV are taken from the Holy Bible, New International Version®, NIV®. Copyright © 1973, 1978, 1984, 2011 by Biblica, Inc.® Used with permission of Zondervan. All rights reserved worldwide. www.zondervan.com. The "NIV" and "New International Version" are trademarks registered in the United States Patent and Trademark Office by Biblica, Inc.®

Verses attributed to J.B. Phillips are taken from The New Testament in Modern English, copyright © 1960, 1972 by J.B. Phillips. Administered by The Archbishops' Council of the Church of England. Used with permission.

Italics in Scripture verses indicate emphasis by author.

Cover design by Bryce Williamson

Cover images © JMGehrke, jeewan chandra, enjoynz / Getty Images

Interior design by KUHN Design Group

For bulk, special sales, or ministry purchases, please call 1-800-547-8979. Email: CustomerService@hhpbooks.com

This logo is a federally registered trademark of the Hawkins Children's LLC. Harvest House Publishers, Inc., is the exclusive licensee of this trademark.

Called to Take a Bold Stand
Copyright © 2025 by Jack Hibbs
Published by Harvest House Publishers
Eugene, Oregon 97408
www.harvesthousepublishers.com

ISBN 978-0-7369-8874-2 (pbk)
ISBN 978-0-7369-8875-9 (eBook)

Library of Congress Control Number: 2024950919

No part of this book may be used or reproduced in any manner for the purpose of training artificial intelligence technologies or systems.

All rights reserved. No part of this publication may be reproduced, stored in a retrieval system, or transmitted in any form or by any means—electronic, mechanical, digital, photocopy, recording, or any other—except for brief quotations in printed reviews, without the prior permission of the publisher.

Printed in the United States of America

25 26 27 28 29 30 31 32 33 / BP / 10 9 8 7 6 5 4 3 2 1

AUTHOR'S DISCLAIMER

It is a safe assumption that what I am calling a disclaimer to you, the reader, is not typical for an author to write. Here is why: I believe it is necessary to acknowledge the importance of two events that converged in a most extraordinary way and ultimately gave birth to the book before you.

The first involves me being a follower of the Lord Jesus Christ for nearly 50 years and receiving a wealth of Christian discipleship and teaching over those decades. Sound biblical doctrine and teaching are responsible for my bold faith in the veracity of the Scriptures and God's promise never to abandon anyone who trusts in Him.

The second is about how *Called to Take a Bold Stand* came to be. It emerged amidst the directives and mandates of so-called experts in the COVID era. During the ensuing drama, one thing was certain: God's Word must be obeyed at all costs as a witness and validation of biblical truth. That steadfast belief led me during those years in both my personal life and as a pastor responsible for the spiritual development of our congregation.

Many people from outside the congregation continue to say they're thankful for the bold stand I took and how my courage remains an inspiration. I feel uncomfortable hearing such words because I am not responsible for what looks like courage to others. I cannot take credit for what took place when it was God all along using His Word in my life. It was an act of sheer obedience to the will of God that led us to leave our church doors open and minister to tens of thousands of people, which has since grown to millions via radio, television, and other media platforms weekly.

In everything that has happened through the ministry at our church, all glory and honor belong to Jesus Christ and His incredible Word, the Bible.

WITH GRATITUDE

Much of the motive for publishing *Called to Take a Bold Stand* is to inspire and encourage the next generation of believers, and those uppermost in my mind are my grandchildren. Emelyn, Oliver, and Ames, you renew my determination to stand for righteousness's sake.

It goes without saying, but I must because of its absolute truthfulness—without my wife Lisa alongside me throughout my decades of ministry, I could not have endured the things that ministry requires of a man. Lisa is an accomplished servant of the gospel in her own right. Her steadfast love for me, knowledge of the Word, and strength in following Jesus have made this book possible.

I would also like to give a very special thanks to the congregation for which I've had the honor of pastoring these 36-plus years. They are my support team of prayer warriors and encouragers. I get attention from the media and others within the Christian community, but it is only because God has allowed me to pastor the most wonderful flock that a shepherd could ask for on this side of heaven.

Thank you to Judi McDaniels, who has been with me through every word, page, and chapter. I am not the easiest person to understand, yet you understood. Your expertise and editorial skills are matchless.

And finally, I want to thank you, the reader. It is your interest in a book such as this that serves as a profound encouragement. As you read what follows in these pages and find your faith being challenged, fortified, and enlarged, it will be because of God's grace as He uses His Word in your life. He alone is faithful.

Awaiting His return,
Jack Hibbs

CONTENTS

Foreword—Franklin Graham 7

PART 1: YOU HAVE WHAT IT TAKES

1. The Real You 13
2. Believe 29
3. Bear His Image 43
4. Remember 59
5. Be Confident 75

PART 2: WATCH OUT

6. Watch and Listen 95
7. In Your Sights 111
8. It's Dark Out There 127
9. Urgent, Urgent, Urgent! 145
10. The False and the True 161

PART 3: GOING PUBLIC

11. What Are You Waiting For? 179
12. Today Is the Best Day 195
13. Heading for Home 211
14. Before I Let You Go 227

Index of Scripture References 243
Notes 249

FOREWORD
FRANKLIN GRAHAM

Benjamin Franklin declared, "Write something worth reading." Jack Hibbs has done this in *Called to Take a Bold Stand*. Pointing to God's Word, he masterfully lays out God's command to be bold and stand fully assured in all the will of God (Acts 4:29; Colossians 4:12).

Have you ever struggled with God's plan and purpose for life, convinced that God's will is a cliffhanger? Many try to uncover the mystery by going to church. Others satisfy themselves by reading a devotional or saying a prayer, hoping it will unlock the riddle. Some believe that doing good deeds to others in the name of Jesus fulfills the will of God. But as Jack points out, God has not hidden His will from us. He clearly tells us, "This is the will of God, your sanctification" (1 Thessalonians 4:3). It is through this journey that we draw closer to Him and His presence in us is revealed: "To them God willed to make known what are the riches of the glory of this mystery…which is Christ in you, the hope of glory" (Colossians 1:27).

The word *sanctification* strikes terror in a lot of people, who believe it to be an archaic process that has no place within our churches and certainly not in our permissive society. Yet today's rap music doesn't cower in using this powerful word while defaming its meaning. But the word *sanctify* is holy and powerfully active. The Bible declares, "Sanctify the Lord God in your hearts" (1 Peter 3:15). This means to be set apart—separated from worldliness—for God's special use and purpose, unashamedly living for Him before an unbelieving world.

This book encourages us to embrace sanctification, not shrink back from it. Jack shares from his heart the thrilling purpose of God's transforming work that calls us to righteous and holy living. We carry within us the abiding presence of His Holy Spirit, leading us to take a bold stand and shine the light of God's truth in what the Bible calls darkened hearts (Romans 1:21).

Confusion about what it means to live for Christ comes from Satan, not from Christ. Satan does not want believers to walk righteously. Why? Because walking in God's righteousness is a strong testimony to His work in us—conforming us to His will. The lines are blurred only to those who are not living obediently in the strength and the truth of God's Word.

The Bible declares, "The grace of God...[teaches] us that, denying ungodliness and worldly lusts, we should live...righteously, and godly in the present age, looking for the blessed hope and glorious appearing of our great God and Savior Jesus Christ, who gave Himself for us, that He might redeem us from every lawless deed and purify for Himself His own special people" (Titus 2:11-14).

When God calls us to be His special people, He uniquely equips us. As believers in Christ, we can walk in God's will knowing that it will lead to inner peace, giving us direction along our pathway and enabling us to live in a way that will bring others to salvation through the saving grace of Jesus Christ alone. This is how we can make a difference here and now in our calling to take a bold stand for Him.

I greatly commend my friend Pastor Jack Hibbs for writing this book. It's needed today because it points us right back to the Bible. God's message to us convicts and comforts, encouraging human hearts and redeemed souls to bear the fruit of sanctification to those who believe, practice, and obey His will.

—**Franklin Graham**
President and CEO
Billy Graham Evangelistic Association
Samaritan's Purse
Boone, North Carolina
February 2025

PART 1

YOU HAVE WHAT IT TAKES

CHAPTER 1

THE REAL YOU

Wars and rumors of wars are one of the signs that Jesus gave regarding the end of the age. Depending on your background, the idea of war will conjure up different images. I was raised in a military family—my dad was a Marine—and I grew up understanding the dynamics of war. But soon after becoming a Christian, I learned that war is not limited to nations fighting one another. There are also spiritual conflicts that manifest themselves in the physical world. That means faith, as the Bible describes it, is at war.

According to the Bible, the Christian's battle is against three great spiritual enemies—the devil, the world, and the flesh. We battle against Satan, our invisible but powerful adversary, the ever-present influence of a fallen world, and the fleshly desires that lurk deep within each of our hearts. All three of these enemies conspire with two primary goals: subdue and conquer.

Clearly identifying the enemy is an all-important component in waging war, but winning it requires a strategy. In developing a strategy, it is wise to use historical facts to form a strong foundation from which to move forward. Military institutions do this by studying history as it pertains to war. I appreciate this dedication because history can tell us about the strengths and weaknesses of combatants, the driving forces behind the conflict, and the way forward to victory. History also shows us where we have come from and where we could be headed if we're not careful.

Once you've done your due diligence, developed a strategy, and confirmed your resources, it is time to take a stand. Why do I stress the need to take a stand? And what kind of stance or position am I referring to? Our biblical beliefs are under full-scale attack, and it is time to take a biblical stand because history teaches that there can be no neutrality when it comes to war. Hostile aggression demands decisive action. For us to be victorious, we must know ourselves and the One who has enlisted us into this bold faith.

YOU ARE CALLED TO STAND

It is hard to imagine World War 2 without the United States's involvement, but it nearly happened. While Hitler's army rolled unchecked through Germany's neighboring countries, US politicians argued about what role, if any, this country should play. Many believed there was no clear mandate for engaging in what they knew would be costly, hard-fought battles. Others thought it best to follow a plan of isolation and appeasement. After all, wasn't it a foreign war?

Despite pleas from its European allies, America waited and watched from a distance. President Franklin Delano Roosevelt's warning, "We well know that we cannot escape danger, or the fear of danger, by crawling into bed and pulling the covers over our heads,"[1] seemed to fall on deaf ears.

Situated between two vast oceans, America believed it could play it safe and remain neutral—until the morning of December 7, 1941. Japan's surprise attack on Pearl Harbor finally ended the debate. War had come to American soil. The following day, Congress declared war on Japan. Germany and Italy—Japan's allies—responded by declaring war against the United States. With evil rising on the other side of both the Atlantic and Pacific, neutrality was no longer a luxury or option. That "foreign war" was now our war. It was time to get involved.

Would history have been different if the US had acted earlier? Considering the horrific loss of life—innocent civilians, soldiers, and the estimated six million Jews who perished—this is a valid question. There is little doubt that the outcomes could have been different.

Today, too much of the professing church resembles America at the start of World War 2—content to look the other way out of fear or apathy or both. When you consider the unwillingness of the church to engage enemies of the gospel inside its walls and outside its gates, the comparison is striking. American leaders could see the warning signs but did not take them seriously. Likewise, some Christians feel that their congregation or organization is insulated or isolated from evil influences, saying, "It'll never happen here." And others believe that through appeasement, they'll be left alone. I think we need to be reminded of Roosevelt's words of warning regarding the futility of hiding because whenever fear disables action, there will be consequences. Like it or not, war has come to our doorstep.

At this moment, the stakes in this all-out war are higher than ever. The time for complacency, as if there ever was one, is long past. It is time to engage those warring against biblical Christianity by taking a bold stand. And by a bold stand, I mean living out a biblically based passionate bold faith—resilient, immovable, and incredibly effective in the last days. Doing anything less neutralizes the church, rendering it ineffective in fulfilling its calling to spread the gospel and make disciples of Jesus Christ. It causes our faith to cease being relevant, useful, or capable of being salt and light. In a word, bold!

Today, the challenge for every Christ-follower is this: Are you willing to take our Lord at His word, believe what He says, and take a stand? Will you decide to make a difference? I urge you to say yes for this reason: However small your efforts may appear, heaven takes a far different view. Believe me when I say that what you do now matters in eternity.

Formulating a strategy for a bold and courageous stand requires a clear understanding of the strength and vitality of what you've become in Christ—the very things you will read in the following pages. We will only scratch the surface of what the Father has afforded us in Christ Jesus, but I pray that what you read galvanizes you into action. As you encounter biblical truth, may you make honest assessments and, when needed, pray, "Lord, please work this characteristic or that way of thinking into my life. From this day forward, help me to never back down or surrender in the fight to uphold the truth of Your Word. O Lord, make me courageous. Help me to develop a bold faith that is equal to taking on these darkening days."

YOU ARE IN CHRIST

When someone turns to you and says, "Look at what you've become," what are they saying? And how are they saying it—with admiration, or sarcasm? Are they witnessing a changed life?

For better or worse, people will make assessments about us based on what they observe regarding our Christianity. That truth should encourage you to ask yourself, *Has my faith changed me?* To help you answer that question, how would your family, friends, or employer say that God has changed you? Those who live with us and around us should experience this firsthand.

If my neighbor texted me a picture of oranges from his tree and asked if I wanted some, I'd say yes because I know they are consistently juicy and flavorful. But suppose he sent me two unremarkable photos, one of a man and the other of a woman, and asked if I would vouch for their character? What could I discern about either of them? Nothing. Could I determine their worldview or what they believe about Jesus? No. Is there anything that I could expect from them? Again, the answer is no. I couldn't expect anything from either of these people because I don't know them.

I cannot determine anything about these two individuals unless I get into their world and live with them. But, if I lived with them 24 hours, seven days a week, for a month, I could tell you a whole lot about each. I could tell you if she's insecure or not. It would be apparent that he's a gamer or mathematically gifted—brilliant, in fact. She likes to paint in her free time, and he plays soccer every weekend. He looked subdued in his picture, but he has a bad temper when pushed. And she has issues when it comes to trusting people.

Now, what if someone stepped into my life? What would they conclude about my Christianity? Do my claims about my faith match what others see? How about yours? When you say that you are a believer, what does that mean? To answer those questions, let's start with what it means doctrinally.

YOU HAVE A NEW NATURE

The title of *Christian* means that you have accepted Jesus Christ as your Lord and Savior. There is no doubt as to His deity; Jesus is both God and Savior. The apostle Paul made this clear in Colossians 1:15-21:

> He is the image of the invisible God, the firstborn over all creation. For by Him all things were created that are in heaven and that are on earth, visible and invisible, whether thrones or dominions or principalities or powers. All things were created through Him and for Him. And He is before all things, and in Him all things consist. And He is the head of the body, the church, who is the beginning, the firstborn from the dead, that in all things He may have the preeminence.

> For it pleased the Father that in Him all the fullness should dwell, and by Him to reconcile all things to Himself, by Him, whether things on earth or things in heaven, having made peace through the blood of His cross.
>
> And you, who once were alienated and enemies in your mind by wicked works, yet now He has reconciled.

Being a Christian means that your faith is in the atoning work of Jesus Christ on the cross for the forgiveness of sins. And like others before you, you can attest, "No good thing dwells in me, but thankfully Jesus died for sinners like me, of which I am chief" (see Romans 7:17; 1 Timothy 1:15).

The moment you acknowledge your personal sins, repent, turn to God, and confess your need before Him, your salvation is secure, and you have "obtained like precious faith with us by the righteousness of our God and Savior Jesus Christ" (2 Peter 1:1). You and I share the exact same precious faith as every single believer who ever came before us and those coming after. God never favors one of His children above another. I want you to notice the definite article *the* in that verse because it tells us why our faith is precious. Our faith is in Jesus' righteousness—His righteousness has become ours—and that makes our faith extremely valuable. The Hope Diamond and all the gold of Fort Knox cannot compare to the value of the faith that has the power to transform you and me.

God sees you and me in a whole new way, and it should be reflected in how we live. In other words, you and I should conduct ourselves in accordance with God's viewpoint and His directives for us. Colossians 3:3 says, "For you died, and your life is hidden with Christ in God." When you came to Christ, you died to the old order of things and faith was born. "As many as received Him, to them He gave the right to become children of God, to those who believe in His name" (John 1:12). Your life is now centered in Christ. He is in full possession of you. When your faith is in Jesus Christ, you are hidden in Him.

One day my grandson was helping me fill a large storage bin with books. Once it was full, I relocated the container to another room, emptied it, and went outside for a few minutes. When I came back inside, I heard my grandson saying, "Papa, Papa." So, I went into the room, but I didn't see him. I could hear him, yet he was nowhere to be seen. Unnoticed by me, he had folded up his arms and legs and climbed inside the bin. He was hidden until out he popped!

I could hear and recognize my grandson's voice even though he was hidden away. When you and I speak, people should recognize our voice, but in a sense, what we say should be coming out of our relationship with Christ. They should hear Jesus and see our lives as a representation of His life lived out through us. That is what it means to be hidden in Christ. "I have been crucified with Christ; it is no longer I who live, but Christ lives in me; and the life which I now live in the flesh I live by faith in the Son of God, who loved me and gave Himself for me" (Galatians 2:20).

Over the years that I've been a pastor, people have told me, "I accepted the Lord ten, twenty, or thirty years ago." And often, my response is, "Great! In those years, have you welcomed the day saying, 'Jesus, here I am? Take all of me'"? If they reply, "Oh no. I don't need to do that. I did that back then," one of my first thoughts is that they might not be a Christ-follower. I wonder if they believed in Jesus only in a historical sense, much like the man who confessed to me, "I believe in Jesus. I own a Bible and go to church. Yet there's been no change in my life. I still drink and use drugs. I still have a temper. And, if I'm honest, I regularly take it out on my spouse. I've alienated my kids. I feel so guilty every day." Ladies and gentlemen, those lifestyle behaviors betray the real message and power of biblical Christianity! They are not biblical or of God.

If you claim to know Christ but you're still living life as you wish, beware. Jesus warned, "Not everyone who says to Me, 'Lord, Lord,' shall enter the kingdom of heaven, but he who does the will of My Father in heaven" (Matthew 7:21). You can protest, "Lord, Lord, have we not prophesied in Your name, cast out demons in Your name, and done many wonders in Your name?" (verse 22). Yet Jesus will declare, "I never knew you; depart from Me, you who practice lawlessness!" (verse 23).

You cannot say you know Jesus and that your life is under His authority and yet have your life remain the same. If Jesus cannot change us from what we used to be, then what is the difference between what He does and what is accomplished through a self-help seminar? But we know there should be a distinct difference in a true believer because Jesus truly changes lives! "If anyone is in Christ, he is a new creation; old things have passed away; behold, all things have become new" (2 Corinthians 5:17).

You've Been Transformed

The prospect of facing spiritual battles can seem daunting, but as a believer, you have what it takes. To prove it to you, let me introduce you to Peter.

Although this isn't a book about the apostle Peter or his words, I often mention both for two reasons. First and foremost, this book is about faith—recognizing what faith is and is not, strengthening it, keeping it, and using it by exercising your spiritual muscles. Peter's grasp of the meaning of true faith is undeniable, especially as it relates to the issues prevalent in today's church. And second, Peter is relatable. I could point out an Old Testament saint like King David—a mighty warrior and writer of poetry—whom God called "a man after My own heart" (Acts 13:22). Or refer to the New Testament apostle Paul, a brilliant intellectual giant. Paul was among the most educated men of the first-century Roman Empire and was seen as one of the greatest converts to Christianity. There are believers today who are of David's renown and Paul's stature, but I believe that most of us find ourselves walking in Peter's sandals much of the time.

According to church history, Simon Peter was a rough, tough, uneducated Galilean fisherman. Scripture tells us that he and his brother Andrew were the first to obey Jesus' call to follow Him (Matthew 4:18-20). And Peter started off with gusto. When the disciples' boat was in the middle of a storm-tossed sea, Peter showed tremendous faith by stepping out of the boat and onto the waves when Jesus invited him to (Matthew 14:29).

Yet if there was an opportunity to misjudge a situation, Peter regularly did. He was impetuous and had a habit of contradicting Jesus. He was passionate, and this often got him in trouble! After Peter promised he would never desert Jesus, he exclaimed, "I do not know the Man!" (Matthew 26:74). Peter's vehement denial could have been the end of his story, but thankfully, for him and us, it wasn't. Peter was lovingly restored by the One whom he had abandoned. And then came the day of Pentecost.

> Being assembled together with them, He commanded them not to depart from Jerusalem, but to wait for the Promise of the Father, "which," He said, "you have heard from Me; for John truly baptized with water, but you shall be baptized with the Holy Spirit not many days from now" (Acts 1:4-5).

Ever since Pentecost, the promised Holy Spirit has indwelled every believer. He is the confirmation stamp, the seal of God's ownership, upon every heaven-bound saint (see 1 Corinthians 6:19; Ephesians 4:30). The Spirit's presence is essential for the Christian life to be effective. When He goes to work in our lives, He strengthens us against temptation, facilitates the operation of our spiritual gifts, and empowers our witness to the world by helping us to live out our faith with boldness.

Following the day of Pentecost (see Acts 2:1-4), the effect of the Holy Spirit on believers was astounding. As you continue to read the book of Acts, there is an incredible download of supernatural inspiration, knowledge, and power in Christ's followers, and we see it first in Peter. The bumbling, impulsive disciple becomes Peter the apostle, a confident and bold messenger of the gospel. Incredibly, 3,000 people were saved following his first public sermon. In the world's eyes, Peter didn't amount to much, but he didn't need to—he was transformed!

Transformation is an incredible word. In the Bible, the Greek term used to describe this is *metamorphoo*, which means a change of condition or form. It suggests that a thorough and dramatic change has taken place. In the life of a believer, transformation is an internal process that begins the moment we become born-again (see John 3:3-8). Nature gives us a physical picture of this spiritual reality through caterpillars. Those hungry little creatures eat their way through your garden until it is time for them to shed their skin and form a chrysalis. Once inside this protective covering, they undergo a complete and radical transformation and emerge as a butterfly or moth. What happens on the inside must eventually manifest itself on the outside in a beautiful way.

Likewise, the transforming power of the Holy Spirit resulted in profound changes within Peter's life. He boldly served Christ and eventually wrote 1 and 2 Peter, books that couldn't be more different in their language and style. First Peter is written in a simple manner, while 2 Peter is technical, advanced, and theologically profound. The sentence structure of 2 Peter reads more like the apostle Paul's writings or what is known as a Pauline style. To some, it seems impossible that an uneducated Galilean penned such lofty words, yet he did.

Peter's continual growth into a deep thinker and fearless defender of the faith came as he yielded himself to the Spirit's work in his life as he immersed himself in the Scriptures.

The practice of immersion is used today by the US military with amazing results. Their renowned language school in Monterey, California, is where they send soldiers whose assignments require them to blend into a foreign region without detection. Through total immersion—not a word of the student's native tongue is spoken or written by the instructor—they learn another country's language, dialect, and ways. Those soldiers know they will be changed by the end of their studies.

Dear saint, when you yielded your life to Jesus, a tremendous change occurred, and the course of your life was forever altered. And because this is true, you are not, and never will be, the same. Now is the time to immerse yourself in God's Word and watch how the Spirit uses it in you!

By God's grace, with the Holy Spirit's help, you are different from where you started in Christ, and you're bringing things like pride, lust, or anger under the control of the Spirit. You are growing in the grace and knowledge of Jesus Christ and advancing in your faith. Second Corinthians 3:18 announces that you are "being transformed…from glory to glory," but this transformation isn't a one-and-done event. It is an ongoing and observable work of the Holy Spirit.

The born-again believer's life has been radically altered—transformed—and with that comes liberation and freedom. Just as a butterfly is liberated from its chrysalis, God has set you free to go out into the world transformed. You are now ready to be used. But the choice about your usefulness to God is yours—you'll see why in a moment.

You've Been Set Free

How do you introduce yourself when you meet someone for the first time? Do you say, "Hi, my name is Paula," or "My name is Bob"? Or is your introduction more like, "I'm Brent, founder and

CEO of the biggest and best construction company in town"? How we view ourselves says a lot about us. Just ask Paul, Timothy, Epaphras, James, Peter, and Jude. Each of these men was a leader within the church, worthy of honor, but first and foremost, they saw themselves as bondservants, or as some Bibles translate it, slaves. In some of their letters to other believers, Peter and Paul even chose to label themselves a bondservant of the Lord Jesus Christ before identifying themselves as an apostle (see Romans 1:1; 2 Peter 1:1).

Coupling the lowly position of a bondservant with that of an esteemed apostle could be considered an oxymoron—two ideas that are in opposition to one another. But in Christ, they come together as a remarkable expression of love.

In ancient history, people were reduced to slavery for various reasons—one of them was debt. If you owed someone money and couldn't repay it, you could bind yourself to that person as a slave until the debt was repaid. Some of these slaves, after completing their time of service, would think, *These years have not been bad. In fact, I like this guy and care for him. He has helped me and my family in so many ways. I don't want to leave him.* So, on the day they could be freed, they went to their master and said, "I don't want to leave you. Under your authority, my life has been better than when I was on my own. Will you have me?"

If the master agreed, he brought the slave to a wooden post. Standing before witnesses, he took the slave's earlobe, placed it against the post, and drove an awl through it. The slave was marked as a bondservant. His decision declared, "I am technically free, but I willingly give my life and freedom back to my master. He is so good" (see Exodus 21:1-6). All of this reflected the deep affection and gratitude of the slave. What followed was a lifelong submission to the will of his master.

Our English word *bondservant* translates to the Greek word *doulos*. Identifying as a *doulos* implies you are already a slave, but you've now plunged headlong into a greater form of slavery. You may be offended at the implication that you are already a slave, but it is true, nonetheless. Undoubtedly, some people will object, "Pastor, you are dead wrong. I do whatever I want. I am my own person and call the shots in my life. I am free." But the Bible disagrees with that assessment. Romans 6:16 says, "Do you not know that to whom you present yourselves slaves to obey, you are that one's slaves whom you obey, whether of sin leading to death, or of obedience leading to righteousness?"

I once watched a news clip of vandals kicking in a vending machine in Toronto, Canada. They beat the machine apart, took all the candy, and ran away shouting, "We're free! We're free!" In their minds, free candy equated to personal freedom, but they weren't free. Their lust for mischief and violence had enslaved them. Their supposed freedom was wrapped in unfettered lawlessness; they had become slaves to anarchy.

You and I may not have been thieves, but in some way, shape, or form, we were slaves to this world and our sinful desires, which are terrible forms of bondage. But after becoming believers, we are now free to serve a different Master.

> Most assuredly, I say to you, whoever commits sin [as a lifestyle] is a slave of sin. And a slave does not abide in the house forever, but a son abides forever. Therefore if the Son makes you free, you shall be free indeed (John 8:34-36).

> The wicked flee when no one pursues, but the righteous are bold as a lion (Proverbs 28:1).

Jesus Christ sets people free forever from the bondage of sin and death. A truly free person lives with great liberty and freedom, abhors wrong, endeavors to do what is right, and experiences a harmonious relationship with God under His rule and reign. This kind of freedom leads believers to become bondslaves in an intimate, free-will act of love.

To a self-seeking person, the idea of holding a position of honor as a child of God but choosing the humble position of a bondservant doesn't make sense. And yet it should because that is what Jesus Himself did:

> Let this mind be in you which was also in Christ Jesus, who, being in the form of God, did not consider it robbery to be equal with God, but made Himself of no reputation, taking the form of a bondservant, and coming in the likeness of men (Philippians 2:5-7).

I urge you to stop and consider the magnitude of what Jesus Christ did for you. The Creator God—sustainer of everything, worthy of all worship, praise, honor, and glory throughout eternity—departed from His throne and entered our humanity. Jesus' decision to make Himself of no reputation rendered Him as nothing in the estimation of men, and He did so willingly.

Jesus *emptied* Himself by laying aside His divine privileges. He, in complete agreement with His Father, embraced what we would call the ultimate humiliation by becoming a human. Jesus never ceased to be God during any part of His earthly ministry when He willingly set aside His heavenly glory. He gladly took on the likeness—the physical characteristics—of a man. Jesus, God incarnate, confined Himself to a human body not for a day or a year, but forever. It is shocking when you consider the implications. At this very hour, Christ, the Son of God, sits at the right hand of God the Father in His glorified human body. He did all this to serve the will of the Father. He did all this for you and me! We are eternally indebted to Jesus. We owe Him everything.

We were not created to be served but to serve. But bear in mind that God never wants us to live as slaves to others. Instead, He desires that Christ's life be lived out by choosing to build up, bless, and serve one another. "Let each of us please his neighbor for his good, leading to edification. For even Christ did not please Himself" (Romans 15:2-3). As an act of love and gratitude for what Christ did for us, let us follow Him.

All of us are slaves, but are you a bondslave of the Lord Jesus Christ? If you are, you will be a doer of God's Word, obedient to your new Master. And when the One who loves you and gave His life for you gives instructions, there will be no debate. You won't go to the left or right. You will follow Him because you are now free to do so.

YOUR TIME IS NOW

By God's design, you are alive at this exact time in history. Many people refer to the space of a person's lifetime as "the dash." When read on a tombstone or in an obituary, the dash looks like 1958–2022. It represents the time God has allotted you on earth and, may I add, the time He has given you to impact others. The psalmist prayed, "Teach us to number our days, that we might gain a heart of wisdom" (Psalm 90:12). Will you ask the same? And what will you say and do during those hours, days, months, and years?

> Now is the time to take a bold stand and turn your world upside down, or better yet, right side up for Jesus' sake.

The Bible says, "Present your members as slaves of righteousness for holiness" (Romans 6:19). The word "members" generally refers to the individual parts that make up our whole body, which definitely applies here. But, in this verse, the Holy Spirit has also arranged the words to convey that every part of us is to be in God's hand as an instrument against evil and unrighteousness.

If you possess the same precious faith that has emboldened Christians throughout history, it is time to take a firm position and engage the culture. Now is the time to take a bold stand and turn your world upside down, or better yet, right side up for Jesus' sake.

CHAPTER 2

BELIEVE

Identity issues have led to polarizing debates within our culture, which, for some, are a rallying cry, and a source of confusion for others. But for the believer, there is no controversy surrounding the reality of who you are in Christ, nor should there be any confusion. The truth of who and what you've become in Him is as clear and indisputable as it is wondrous.

Of course, you can neglect your new identity to your detriment, but identifying as a Christ-follower should define everything about you. He has altered the course of your life, and you are on a new path filled with God's purposes.

A true sense of purpose influences how we live because, without real direction or meaning, we tend to drift aimlessly, never finding true satisfaction. Sadly, many people live like that, and frustration and despair are the unfortunate results. I don't believe that a born-again believer can or should live without the knowledge of God's plans for them. While it is impossible to anticipate all that God has in store for you, knowing that He has a plan should fill you with excitement, awe, and energizing faith!

GOD'S PURPOSES COME WITH PROMISES

It is easy to believe that God knows everything there is to be known yet overlook the implications for our life. The Lord told the prophet Jeremiah, "Before I formed you in the womb I knew you; before you were born I sanctified you; I ordained you a prophet to the nations" (Jeremiah 1:5). Personally, I live my life by that verse because God's foreknowledge and preordained plans are not limited to prophets—they include you and me.

God's eternal thoughts and plans for us are simply too numerous to comprehend. The psalmist pointed out the enormity of God's thoughts and plans for us when he wrote,

> Your eyes saw my substance, being yet unformed.
> And in Your book they all were written,
> the days fashioned for me,
> when as yet there were none of them.
> How precious also are Your thoughts to me, O God!
> How great is the sum of them!
> If I should count them, they would be more in number
> than the sand;
> when I awake, I am still with You (Psalm 139:16-18).

I find it significant that these remarkable verses don't mention our natural abilities. And it's for this reason: God has already furnished a lavish supply of everything we need to live confidently.

Like all believers, we were set apart by God "before the foundation of the world" (Ephesians 1:4) for a reason and a purpose. "We are His workmanship, created in Christ Jesus for good works, which God prepared beforehand that we should walk in them" (Ephesians 2:10). The word "workmanship" is translated from the Greek word *poiema*, or work of art. This is where we get our word *poem*. But it could also refer to a song, painting, or some type of grand architecture. This is how God sees you and me! Imperfect and in progress? Yes, but in God's eyes, a masterpiece of great value and worth. Being His workmanship doesn't mean we get to lounge around for all to admire, because with privilege comes responsibility.

God knew exactly where you would go in life and where you would be at the time of reading this book. He molded and shaped you and steered you down specific paths to reach this point. One day you will be in heaven, but until then, you've received a mandate, a commission concerning the kingdom of God, and the ability to carry it out.

To the doubter who thinks, *That's well and good for so-and-so, but you don't know how little I have to offer,* allow me to illustrate an important point. You wouldn't see much if I pulled out my wallet and opened it. I don't carry cash, but I do have a piece of plastic, a credit card with my name imprinted on it. In some ways, my identity in the world is connected to the name on that card. Now, my name might mean something at my bank, but the card's real value is tied to the resources behind my name. Yet the truth is that what I possess is a speck of dust compared to the vast and incalculable resources behind the name of Jesus Christ.

If ever there was someone who could believe that they brought something of value to the table, spiritually speaking, it would be the apostle Paul. Yet Paul's contrast of God's sufficiency versus the inadequacy of man's resources gives us a much-needed perspective.

> We are to God the fragrance of Christ among those who are being saved and among those who are perishing. To the one we are the aroma of death leading to death, and to the other the aroma of life leading to life. And who is sufficient for these things? (2 Corinthians 2:15-16).

> Not that we are sufficient of ourselves to think of anything as being from ourselves, but our sufficiency is from God (2 Corinthians 3:5).

> He [the Lord] said to me, "My grace is sufficient for you, for My strength is made perfect in weakness." Therefore most gladly I will rather boast in my infirmities, that the power of Christ may rest upon me (2 Corinthians 12:9).

Believer, your resources rest solely on God's "exceedingly great and precious promises" (2 Peter 1:4), each backed by the strength and power of the Promise Keeper. Scholars have estimated that there are more than 7,400 promises in the Bible designed to inform and sustain you throughout your life!

The older I get, the more cautious I am with making promises. When I was young, I made promises all the time, and I fully intended to keep them. Or at least I *believed* I would be able to keep them, only to discover that I didn't always have the power to follow through. I am not saying that we shouldn't promise to do certain things because many parts of life operate on the assurance that we'll keep our word. My point is that you discover whether someone will keep their word only when that pledge is tested. The intention behind a promise can be sincere, but then circumstances intervene, and suddenly, the promise is broken. Humans fail. God never does.

Now, I've heard people accuse God of failing to keep His word. They will say things like, "I believed a promise in the Bible, but God didn't come through." Or "I prayed. I've stood upon His Word. And nothing happened." Yet as we seek the fulfillment of God's promises, we must take into account the duration, the time that it takes for something to occur, and endurance, the fortitude to wait upon God's response.

Our timeline is almost always different than God's. He gives a promise at point A, but He knows that its fulfillment goes all the way to points L, M, N, O, and P. On our end, when God's response takes much longer than we expected, we become impatient and sometimes petulant. But when God eventually does what He said He would do, what does that tell you about His promises? He is faithful, even in the waiting. And you can look back and see how all the pieces fit together perfectly to bring you to this point.

GOD PROMISES:

You Are Complete

You might not feel like it, but the Bible says that God has made you complete in Christ. "You are complete in Him, who is the head of all principality and power" (Colossians 2:10). The sufficiency that you read about in previous verses enables you to be all you're supposed to be and to fulfill your purpose, to His glory. God does that by supplying an abundance of what you need to carry you through life. Second Peter 1:2-3 tells us what this entails: "Grace and peace be multiplied to you in the knowledge of God and of Jesus our Lord, as His divine power has given to us all things that pertain to life and godliness, through the knowledge of Him who called us by glory and virtue." Grace and peace multiplied. Wow! God has *already* provided an abundance of grace and peace.

Imagine an ample supply of God's divine favor resting upon you throughout life and peace that is ready and waiting to be experienced in extreme situations and mundane annoyances alike. Yet, whenever you and I do not experience God's peace, we are not resting in what He has already provided. We have allowed someone or something to take us in another direction. I had this brought home to me while driving to a funeral.

I was late, which isn't a big deal to some, but from my earliest years, my parents instilled in me the principle that if you don't arrive early, you are late. In this case, I was late because I trusted my car's navigation system to get me to my destination. The voice of my GPS told me to turn left in 300 feet, so I turned left. I'm not sure why, but I was soon instructed to make a U-turn and head back in the direction I came from. The GPS continued making unreasonable requests until I lost patience and demanded, "What is wrong with you?" The problem was that I was depending on false information to get where I needed to go, making me not only late but anxious and irritable enough to rebuke a device.

When it comes to taking direction for our lives, we cannot take guidance from any source other than the Bible. Doing so only leads to frustration. We must let God's Word settle down into our souls because, through Scripture, we are made "complete, thoroughly equipped for every good work" (2 Timothy 3:16-17). You and I can live powerful Christian lives by believing and appropriating all God has lavishly supplied beforehand.

Sometimes, I wonder if God is looking down from heaven and thinking, *That person loves and says they trust Me. They've put faith in My Son, and My Spirit is upon them. If only they would take what I've supplied that pertains to godliness, righteousness, and virtue and by the grace they've received, just go out and live it.*

Parents are familiar with this kind of thinking, and they get frustrated when a child has it within themselves to accomplish something, but they say, "Mom, Dad, I can't do it." Parents usually counter with, "Yes, you can." Now think about the times you've said something like that to your heavenly Father. "I can't live like that. I can't do, think, or be like that. I can't be joyful or happy in You alone."

I cannot say this strongly enough: Believe God's Word! Tomorrow morning, take God at His word and ask Him to use you. I am confident that the world you encounter will be transformed somehow. The change may be large or small, seen or unseen, but I assure you, it will be there. That confidence isn't based on my opinion, nor should yours be. Our confidence must be in the Holy Spirit, who will use any man or woman yielded to the will of the Father. You have complete confidence that God will take you to heaven. Now, walk confidently in what He has supplied for you: grace and peace multiplied! Sure, you might stumble a time or two, but don't let that stop you. Get up, dust yourself off, and keep going.

The ability to appropriate grace and peace comes from the knowledge, *epiginosko*, of God. *Epiginosko* is a funny-sounding but incredible Greek word. It isn't based on head knowledge, but rather, a knowledge of God that is experiential. It refers to when you, the believer, experience God's nature in real life.

Notice that I said experiential, not experimental. There are hangars at a nearby municipal airport that house airplanes labeled experimental. I love to fly, but I don't advise getting into anything that says experimental on it. Why? Because they're still working out the bugs. These aircraft haven't been certified for standard airworthiness. The engineers or builders can't guarantee that the systems will work consistently 100 percent of the time. They're iffy. But unlike those aircraft, the object of your faith is not still being worked on. It is finished, waiting for you to experience it on a day-to-day basis through a deep, personal relationship with the knowable God. No other religion can make that claim—not Islam, Hinduism, Buddhism, Mormonism, or New Ageism.

The gods connected with those religious systems are aloof and unknowable by their followers, unlike Yahweh, who sent His Son so that we might experience Him personally. When Philip asked Jesus to "show us the Father," Jesus replied, "Have I been with you so long, and yet you have not known Me, Philip? He who has seen Me has seen the Father" (John 14:8-9).

John 17:3 connects eternal life (future) and experiencing God (now) together in a precious way: "This is eternal life, that they may know You, the only true God, and Jesus Christ whom You have sent." The reality of eternal life begins at the moment of salvation. You don't have to wait for it. How can I be so sure? Because you have the assurance of experiencing God as only His children can.

You Are Family

Family ties are important, but many of those relationships are far from ideal. Some of you come from homes where broken promises and commitments were all you knew. Or perhaps, like many, you are tempted to let a difficult relationship with a parent affect your relationship with God. I have been guilty of this at times, which is why I am thankful that the Holy Spirit bears witness that we've been adopted into a new family with a new Father. We are in God's family now! Romans 8:15-16 tells us, "You [have] received the Spirit of adoption by whom we cry out, 'Abba, Father.' The Spirit Himself bears witness with our spirit that we are children of God." What a profound statement with far-reaching implications!

Under ancient Judaism, adoption was primarily reserved for males and used to preserve a family's bloodline. But when Paul wrote to the predominately non-Jewish believers in Rome, "God has chosen to call you His own—He has adopted you," they understood what he meant. They were now a part of God's family and could call Him their Papa.

According to Roman law, you could pick whoever you wanted—male or female—to inherit your wealth and power, and through adoption, all your rights and privileges became theirs. To make the adoption process official, both parties would stand before seven eyewitnesses. The soon-to-be parent would place his hand on the head of the adoptee and say, "This is my only son or daughter." From the moment the person made that declaration in front of the witnesses, they were vowing to uphold their commitment to the life of that young man or woman. It was what the Roman emperor Julius Caesar did for Gaius Octavius. Julius Caesar had no heirs, but Gaius Octavius so impressed him that he determined to adopt the young man.

Adoption changed the newly renamed Gaius Julius Caesar's life forever, just as it has changed yours.

If you are Jewish, calling God your Papa probably seems offensive. Similarly, when believers claim to have a close, intimate relationship with God, it greatly offends legalistic people who will say, "That's sacrilegious." Maybe it is for them, but not for God's sons and daughters. It's no different than watching the kids in Israel today playing and goofing off and calling out to their dads, saying, "Abba," or as the Italians would say, "Papa, Papa!"

What's great about being a child is that no matter what happens in your family, you will always be part of it. I don't know about you, but when I was growing up, childhood friends sometimes teased, "Guess what? Your brother or sister told me that you were adopted." That friend was inferring that you didn't really belong in your family, and the mockery stung if you believed them. Their insinuation was that adoption is awful. But once you learn that you get to heaven by being adopted, suddenly, adoption is terrific. "Sign me up!" you say. "God, please adopt me into Your family."

In a family, there should be no difference between the kids or grandkids born into the family and any who are adopted. I have an adopted grandchild who is no different than the other grandchildren, so much so, that I forget that they are adopted! From a biblical standpoint, for us to be adopted is special because we're called out and chosen to be brought into the family, which is what God did for you and me. "God decided in advance to adopt us into His own family by bringing us to Himself through Jesus Christ. This is what He wanted to do, and it gave Him great pleasure" (Ephesians 1:5 NLT).

We have all made plans for our lives without fully knowing who we are, what we're supposed to be, or where we will go. But our heavenly Father knows. As one of His own, you get to experience all the rights, privileges, and benefits of His kingdom, along with unfettered access to His throne in time of need (see Hebrews 4:16). God has given you exceedingly abundantly more than you can think or ask of Him! (Ephesians 3:20).

His Nature Is in You

Outside of Christianity, nothing in this universe offers humanity a loving, forgiving, holy, righteous, all-powerful God who says, "If anyone loves Me, he will keep My word; and My Father will love him, and We will come to him and make Our home with him" (John 14:23). And who also says, "You will be a partaker of My divine nature" (see 2 Peter 1:4). Some people are shocked when they read Peter's statement that they can be "partakers of the divine nature," and I understand why because these words are heavy with meaning.

Jesus promises that once your name is written in the Lamb's Book of Life, He will never blot it out (Revelation 3:5). The reason why this is true is because the Holy Spirit has deposited the divine nature into every true believer, never to be removed. You escaped the judgment you rightly deserved, the blood of Jesus Christ paid the penalty for your sins, and as a result, you are eternally secure. This should inspire within you a sense of bold confidence for both now and the future.

As a partaker of the divine nature, you are not a little god, but you do begin acting like God by manifesting His characteristics—"love, joy, peace, longsuffering, kindness, goodness, faithfulness, gentleness, self-control" (Galatians 5:22-23). Displaying the characteristics of God is living out your faith with the Holy Spirit as your source of power. That, my friend, is encouraging! We get worn out and frustrated. He never does. God is energetically active, fervent, tirelessly at work in us.

Philippians 2:13 tells us, "It is God who works in you both to will and to do for His good pleasure." In the original Greek text, the word "in" is translated from *en,* which means firmly fixed within, firmly positioned in both place and time; the context is within a person. In its technical form, *en* indicates a separation, direction, and action that is hard to understand but able to be observed. Connected to *en* is another word from the New Testament Greek that is familiar to modern ears, especially those who enjoy physical exercise. The English translation of this Greek word is *elliptical*—an ongoing orbit or circular action within a course or track.

Put these two words—*en* and *elliptical*—together, and you are able to better understand what "God who works in you" means. God has bolted Himself down inside of you, never to be dislodged. Your salvation is signed, sealed, and secure! And when God goes to work, He puts you on a track and sets your life on a course that is sometimes difficult to understand. But keep at it! No matter how slow the pace, keep moving, just as you would on an elliptical machine.

When you grasp onto the truth that God's Spirit is at work in and through you, your life will change. You will find yourself following the exhortations in Psalm 37:3-4: "Trust in the LORD, and do good; dwell in the land, and feed on His faithfulness. Delight yourself also in the LORD, and He shall give you the desires of your heart."

The acts of trusting, dwelling, feeding, and delighting are all part of a closer relationship with the Lord. As you draw closer and closer to God, you will desire what He desires. You will agree more and more with Him and see things the way He sees them. You will speak the way God speaks, love what He loves, and hate what He hates. God's plans will become yours. When God's Spirit is at work, you benefit, He is glorified, and the pressure to perform goes away.

Now can you see why it's not what *you* can do but what the *Spirit* does in and through you that matters?

You Will Not Be Ashamed

Almost nothing is private about Christianity except perhaps our first confession of faith in Jesus Christ as Lord. But eventually, faith brings forth evidence that we are submitting to God's love and plans for us. I hope and trust that you are beginning to see what God intends for you. God woke me up to the reality of forgiveness of sins and faith in Christ when I was 19 years old. Ever since that day, I have known His presence in every situation, good and bad. And this is what I've learned: God wants us to grow through every circumstance, which is why Scripture exhorts us to give all diligence to add virtue to our faith (2 Peter 1:5).

Virtue is an interesting word in the original Greek text. The word is *areté*, which was associated with the name of the ancient Greek god Ares. Ares was the god of war, which shades the idea of virtue with a different hue than what we're used to. In the Western world, we think of virtue in the sense of morality and character, but in this context, it goes beyond that. Virtue, in this sense, doesn't mean polite or nice. It means to possess tenacity, moral courage, and a warrior strength that is submissive to biblical doctrine rather than feelings.

Biblical virtue is under attack today. Again, I am not referring to a type of morality. I'm talking about virtue that causes you to take a stand. For instance, murder: Is it right or wrong? It's wrong. Are you sure? Evangelist Ray Comfort tells the story of an English woman who had Alzheimer's disease. Her son was tired of seeing her suffer, so he threw her off a balcony, and she died. When he was put on trial, the court ruled his action to be one of the most merciful it had ever seen. Ray took the news article onto American university campuses and asked. "What would you do in that situation?" Shockingly, an overwhelming number of people said killing her was the right thing to do because she was suffering.[1]

What about abortion, the killing of babies? The fight for the right to abort unborn children is fraught with emotional appeals that have no biblical basis. If you stand in defense of these vulnerable lives, you will need virtue. You will need tenacity and courage when you're threatened and mocked and ridiculed for taking a bold stand.

When someone comes against your values in the public square, you need to stand strong. But first, you want to make sure that you know why you hold a particular position. No one should ever take a stand based on the views of their pastor, famous religious leader, or conservative political pundit. You might ask, "Aren't we supposed to follow informed godly examples?" Yes, of course. But that is not the kind of conviction that translates into moral courage. You must know the foundations upon which your beliefs are based. I know mine and often hear people say, "You're so dogmatic and stubborn." That's not entirely true. I am only dogmatic and stubborn about matters I am fully convinced of. So when you say, "I'll never budge on this topic because I've done my due diligence and thoroughly researched it," I'll say, "Good for you. You have a clear understanding as to what you are fighting for."

You need to stand for what you know is absolute truth. When you are holding fast in the battle, you can be assured of better things to come. I know this to be true because that's one of God's precious promises.

> They cried to You, and were delivered;
> they trusted in You, and were not ashamed (Psalm 22:5).

> Let me not be ashamed;
> let not my enemies triumph over me.
> Indeed, let no one who waits on You be ashamed;
> let those be ashamed who deal treacherously without
> cause (Psalm 25:2-3).

> Scripture says, "Whoever believes on Him will not be
> put to shame" (Romans 10:11).

The Hebrew word translated "ashamed" means delayed, humiliated, or ridiculed. But remember that God does not frustrate His children. Though people will come against you in all sorts of ways, keep your head up and look up—all will be well in the end. There is a day coming when you will stand before the Lord at the judgment seat of Christ and none of the shame of this world will be upon you. "We must all appear before the judgment seat of Christ, that each one may receive the things done in the body, according to what he has done, whether good or bad" (2 Corinthians 5:10).

In the Greek text, a single word, *bema*, is used for "judgment seat." This is not the great white throne judgment found in Revelation 20:11-15. There, God will judge the unbelieving world, and after their judgment, they will then be escorted into hell. If you are a Christian, you are not going there. Your salvation was settled at the cross; you are no longer under the condemnation of sin (Romans 8:1). The judgment seat of Christ has nothing to do with the issue of salvation, but rather, rewards. As a believer, you will stand before Jesus at the *bema* seat. In ancient times, a *bema* seat was a raised platform from which judges viewed athletic contestants. This is where the modern-day Olympic games got the idea for the platforms on which athletes receive their gold, silver, and bronze medals.

When Jesus judges the church at the *bema* seat, He will judge you and me individually. He will assess our thoughts, motives, and actions, and reward us based on our faithfulness to what He called us to do. I guarantee that on that day, you will stand before the Lord with gladness for the times when God worked in and through your life—including times in which you might not have been aware that He was using you!

We must never forget that faith is the foundation where we must start and that faith must grow and be seen because Christianity, according to the Bible, is visible, public, and active. Christ's followers are to be ablaze in the darkness of this age. The hour has come, and the need is great for us to burn as bright lights in this world.

Live out your calling, and I guarantee you'll learn that God will give you everything you need to carry out His plans for you. He will be the One to perfect and complete all that concerns you (Psalm 138:8)—because what we do here and now matters!

CHAPTER 3

BEAR HIS IMAGE

God's creation has always fascinated me and my family. From the squirrel's antics to the invasions of birds and butterflies in our yard, we see God's handiwork. And when we travel, we take every opportunity to explore nature, so visiting the giant sequoias of California on our way to an out-of-state wedding made sense.

California is home to the oldest, tallest, and largest trees on the planet. These trees are impressive, especially the Sequoia National Park's General Sherman Tree. Though estimated to be between 2,300 and 2,700 years old, it's not California's oldest tree. That distinction goes to Methuselah, a 4,850-year-old bristlecone pine tree. Located in a remote area between California's Sierra Nevada mountains and the Nevada state border, Methuselah is considered to be the oldest living thing on Earth.

General Sherman is also not the tallest. The coastal redwood Hyperion tops out at over 380 feet. But while General Sherman is not the oldest or tallest, it is the largest tree by volume on the planet—nothing is bigger than this behemoth. Standing 275 feet tall with a 36-foot circumference, it consumes 1,000 gallons of water every 24 hours. General Sherman's bark grows at a rate that equals a 60-foot ponderosa pine every year. Some say you can almost hear the massive giant growing.

It is hard to believe, but General Sherman's life began with a tiny seed the size of a pinhead. When that seed fell into the ground and died, it initiated the growth we see today. Stored within Sherman's seed was the DNA data it needed to advance toward maturity until it became the fulfillment of what God designed it to be. I cannot think of a better picture of the sanctification process of growth in the believer's life.

BEARING HIS IMAGE BY GROWING

I believe that at the inception of our conversion, every Christian has a Holy Spirit-imprinted DNA that prompts you and me to grow. Unlike the seed, we could not die for the atonement of our sins, but Jesus did. Jesus saves. He forgives. He redeems. And Jesus sanctifies. From that starting point, Christ starts the germination of spiritual DNA—an explosion of spiritual information—that causes a day-by-day dynamic relationship between us and God.

Christian, your life with Christ began with one simple cry to the Lord Jesus Christ—"O Lord, save me!"—and faith was awakened. There was a germination of spiritual enlightenment, and thoughts of God began percolating deep within. Pursuing truth, the meaning of life, and a knowledge of God became important. Now, you walk with God through times of rich blessing and heart-wrenching storms, much like the sequoias, which weather torrential downpours while waiting for sunnier days. Eventually, those seasons pass into years, and when your life reaches its conclusion, you are as God has designed. What is happening? Sanctification—growth in Christ that brings about a spiritually complete person.

Sanctification is fantastic because you cannot help but feel a sense of awe when you look back at what God has done. When I stood in that sequoia grove, many of the visitors were whispering. I asked one lady why, and she reverently said, "Because it's awesome. How'd they get so big?" Do you ever look at what God has done and is doing in your life? I know I do. I expected to be more patient and loving by now, but the truth is that I can see God still at work in me.

I am saddened when I hear of Christians whose growth is stunted. Many have been believers for years but are stuck, still fretting over their salvation. They haven't moved on to deeper doctrines, which is a shame. God wants them to move on from the basic principles of Christ and mature (Hebrews 6:1-2) because sanctification has past, present, and future realities. Let me share with you three verses to help you understand why this is true.

Ephesians 2:8

"By grace you have been saved through faith, and that not of yourselves; it is the gift of God." The phrase "have been" is past tense. Your salvation could have happened minutes, years, or decades ago, but it is now past, and you are wonderfully saved. It's time to move into the present and experience all that God has for you.

1 Corinthians 1:18

"The message of the cross is foolishness to those who are perishing, but to us who are being saved it is the power of God." When the Bible says we are "being saved," it doesn't mean our salvation is in jeopardy. It means that salvation is being worked out in our lives, and the evidence of it can be measured—like the growth produced by the many gallons of water sequoias drink daily. Drink deeply of God's Word, and you will grow. It happens naturally.

Romans 5:9

"Much more then, having now been justified by His blood, we shall be saved from wrath through Him." The promise of "shall be saved from wrath" is yet future. The inside of you is redeemed (saved), and hopefully, you are displaying proof of your new identity, but there is one more thing needed for this trinity of truth to be complete. One day, at either the trumpet blast of the rapture of the New Testament church or the call of God upward in death, your body will be transformed in "the twinkling of an eye" (1 Corinthians 15:52). This is the culmination of God's redemptive act—you will be saved from the wrath yet to come.

The everyday details of sanctification look different in each believer's life, but God is entirely committed to the process. "For this is the will of God, your sanctification" (1 Thessalonians 4:3). To "sanctify" a vessel or object is to set it apart for special use, and to "sanctify" a person is to make them holy. Positionally, God now sees us as holy because of the blood of Jesus. But the Bible also refers to sanctification as a practical ongoing separation from the world and unto God. Through sanctification, God gradually removes from us the controlling passions of this world and replaces them with a Christ-centered way of living. It is God's work in which we cooperate.

When you focus on Christ, thoughts of *Grab all the gusto you can*, and *Eat, drink, and be merry, for tomorrow we die* go out the window. It also does away with the assumption that, because I gave my heart to Jesus and He forgave all my sins, I can do whatever I want, guilt-free. That, my friend, is called antinomianism—a big word that means you believe you can sin up a storm, and because God is so good, He'll forgive your sins when you run back to Him asking for forgiveness, even while you have the intent to repeat the cycle again.

Antinomianism is a horrific theological lie. It is how people wind up in hell. Why? Because they've made a confession or profession of faith, but there is no day-to-day active change in their life. There is no evidence of the sanctification that occurs with true salvation. If that is you, and you only want comfort and ease, go to your local furniture store and pick out a new mattress. Do you just want to have fun? Visit an amusement park. But if you desire to walk with Christ, put in your mouthpiece and strap on your helmet.

When I look out at the congregation at my church, I see men and women who have gone or are currently going through incredible difficulties. In the short term, it would've been far easier not to become a Christian. But they gave their heart to Jesus, and the sanctifying process began. They've been growing in Christ, and when the temptation came to give up or give in, they said, "Lord, to whom shall we go? You have the words of eternal life" (John 6:68).

The reality is that the Christian life is hard, yet we shouldn't want to exchange it for anything. How long will it be hard? Until the day we die, and that day will be awesome because it's graduation day! For those who never accept Christ, this life is as close to heaven as they'll ever get. It's true that they'll enjoy the beauty and benefits that exist here on Earth, yet this is as good as it gets. But for the believer, this is as close to hell as they'll ever get, and what awaits is glory far beyond man's imagination.

A.W. Tozer, in his book *The Knowledge of the Holy*, wrote a statement that I believe is worth considering here: "What comes into our minds when we think about God is the most important thing about us…Worship is pure or base as the worshiper entertains high or low thoughts of God."[1] That is a great quote and 100 percent true. What you think about God matters tremendously and affects how you pursue living for Him or don't. Now let's add a statement from C.S. Lewis: "How God thinks of us is not only more important but is infinitely more important. Indeed, how we think of Him is of no importance except insofar as it is related to how He thinks of us."[2] These two quotes seem to oppose one another when, in reality, they are symbiotic, meaning they are mutually related.

God has touched our lives, and the thoughts we think about Him become the most important thoughts we have. They confirm that in Christ Jesus, God loves us and has fully committed Himself to us. How can we offer Him anything less? "I beseech you therefore, brethren, by the mercies of God, that you present your bodies a living sacrifice, holy, acceptable to God, which is your reasonable service. And do not be conformed to this world, but be transformed by the renewing of your mind, that you may prove what is that good and acceptable and perfect will of God" (Romans 12:1-2).

BEARING HIS IMAGE BY BEING FRUITFUL

We must stop resisting God's work and lean into the Christian experience. We need to roll up our sleeves, get involved, and yield to what He wants to accomplish in and through us. When God says, "I want you to do this or that," we must cooperate with Him. How will we know what we're to do? Stay in the Bible. It's all in God's Word. Jesus illustrated this by saying,

> I am the vine, you are the branches. He who abides in Me, and I in him, bears much fruit; for without Me you can do nothing…If you abide in Me, and My words abide in you, you will ask what you desire, and it shall be done for you. By this My Father is glorified, that you bear much fruit; so you will be My disciples (John 15:5, 7-8).

The promise "If you abide in Me, and My words in you" is as convicting as much as it is compelling. None of us have arrived when it comes to yielding our lives. There is always more of us to surrender. But, when we abide in the life-giving Word, God's life flows into ours, enabling us to become fruitful disciples. A great companion passage to John 15 is 2 Peter 1:5-8:

> For this very reason, giving all diligence, add to your faith virtue, to virtue knowledge, to knowledge self-control, to

self-control perseverance, to perseverance godliness, to godliness brotherly kindness, and to brotherly kindness love. For if these things are yours and abound, you will be neither barren nor unfruitful in the knowledge of our Lord Jesus Christ.

Peter's exhortation should cause us to sit up and take notice. The prospect of adding these Christian graces to our lives promises tremendous joy, but it also carries a grave warning—don't become unfruitful because of complacency in our Christian profession.

God designed us to grow, yet we are responsible for responding. The words "giving" and "diligence" in 2 Peter 1:5 are action words. You and I are called to cast ourselves fully—100 percent, our whole person—upon what God has already supplied. In the previous chapter, we saw that we are to add knowledge to virtue and that knowledge is experiential. Here, I want to expound a bit more on experiencing God.

God draws near to you as you draw near to Him (James 4:8). Allow His Word to fill your mind and direct your will. The closer you are to the Lord, the more you'll experience His presence, leading to greater satisfaction in life. Will there be goosebumps? Nope. How about feelings? Not necessarily, because in everything, doctrine sets the standard. But you will know spiritual power.

Some will say we shouldn't emphasize experience because it leads people astray. I understand that, but as God sanctifies you and me in our Christian walk, we are experiencing Him—often in the simplest and most basic ways. Perhaps while you are mowing the lawn, a mental light goes on regarding something from your Bible reading, and your thoughts turn toward God. Or you are out and about, and you find yourself looking where you shouldn't. Instantly, you sense in your heart, *Don't look that way; turn away*, and you obey. And this next example is one I'm guilty of. I'm driving and listening intently to a podcast or message, so I'm not paying attention to the speed limit until I sense the Lord saying, "Take it easy. Slow down. Let your foot off the pedal." What is going on in these instances? You are experiencing the sanctifying work of God's Spirit in your life.

Self-Controlled Perseverance

In addition to knowledge, 2 Peter 1:5 says to give "all" diligence to pursuing self-control, which is a fruit of the Spirit. What does "all" mean? It means ALL. We are to put forth every effort to the mastery of ourselves. You are to master you. I'm to master me. We're to master our passions and desires, and therein lies the struggle. Self-control requires the commitment to persevere and push on when everything seems against us, we are tired, and we want to quit. Don't do it! The Holy Spirit gives us the power to resist that urge with no strings attached. That power is ours by pure grace.

Godliness and Brotherly Kindness

It is time to take hold of what God has already supplied and add to your faith godliness, brotherly kindness, and love (2 Peter 1:7). Personal piety is a mark of godliness, but there is a prerequisite. It is a righteousness that mimics God. Ephesians 5:1 says, "Therefore be imitators of God as dear children." Does that sound difficult? It's not. Imitating God implies we have a heart to do it, which God supplies us.

Let God use you by imitating what His Son did. Jesus said, "I do nothing of Myself; but as My Father taught Me, I speak these things. And He who sent Me is with Me. The Father has not left Me alone, for I always do those things that please Him" (John 8:28-29).

Some situations demand us to ask, "Based on the Bible, what would Jesus do right now?" And a great way to start your day is by asking Him, before your feet touch the ground in the morning, "What do You want me to pursue today, Jesus?"

When we see Jesus' actions and attitudes in the Gospels, we're to get up and be like Him in this world. Despite feelings or personal costs, we must decide to do what Jesus would in every situation and place. This is how you take your faith out of the box, so to speak, and experience the vibrant Christian walk that God intends.

Being devoted to choosing God's desires is sanctification in practice. All He calls us to do is offer a willing, yielded heart. And all we need to say is, "Lord, do Your work in my life." It's that simple. Amazing, isn't it?

God may call you to exercise godliness in a corporate corner office, at your family's kitchen table, or both. The location doesn't matter. The people do. Is there someone you have a hard time being around? Someone that you just don't like—maybe your feelings even border on disgust? Here is what you need to do: Single them out as a target of God's affection and show them brotherly kindness—the same warm friendliness you would show a friend. At first, doing this will be hard, then clumsy, but by your third and fourth attempts, you'll start to see power in your actions. And guess what? When you start acting like you like someone, you wind up genuinely caring for and eventually loving that person. But if you let those negative feelings continue to fester, you'll end up with an ugly mess. Thank God that He shows us a better way!

Greater Love

Scripture tells us that "God is love" (1 John 4:16), and because we want to imitate Him, we must love as He loves. But what does that mean? Unfortunately, our English language is somewhat deficient when it comes to the word *love*. We have only one word to describe the many types of love we experience. We love ice cream, spectacular sunsets, puppy breath, and a baby's smile, yet each is so different as not to be comparable. But the New Testament uses various words for the different types of love we experience. The greatest love is *agape*, God's supernatural outpouring of love for you and me.

Agape is the epitome of love, its highest expression, and what we are commanded to show one another (Mark 12:31). Even though agape love is perfectly defined in 1 Corinthians 13, we often struggle with extending it to others. Here is why: We must *choose* it. Like all the previous virtues I've mentioned, we must choose to let God work His divine love through us.

Agape loves in situations where there seems to be no love left or where there was never any to begin with. Agape even loves the enemy who is plotting our destruction. None of us should throw our hands up in disgust or fear and say, "I've lost all hope." Not while we can call upon the love of God.

> In this the love of God was manifested toward us, that God has sent His only begotten Son into the world, that we might live through Him. In this is love, not that we loved God, but that He loved us and sent His Son to be the propitiation for our sins. Beloved, if God so loved us, we also ought to love one another (1 John 4:9-11).
>
> What is important is faith expressing itself in love (Galatians 5:6 NLT).

Agape isn't something that the world understands. When nonbelievers hear Christians say, "I love you, and that's why I want to tell you about Jesus," they think, *You're kidding me. How can you love someone you don't know?* But you know it's true. You love that person because God burdened your heart for that individual. The thought of their hellish future turns your stomach. That, my friend, is agape love. God freely loved you, and now you can't wait to share His mercy and grace with others because the love of Christ compels you (2 Corinthians 5:14). If the world saw the love of Jesus in the way we loved them, I believe they would knock down the doors of our churches to get inside.

As you look at the fruit I mentioned—self-control, perseverance, godliness, brotherly kindness, and love—you might say to yourself, "I'm such a failure." King David felt that way too. He was a man who knew God and was blessed by Him, yet he slept with another man's wife. When Bathsheba realized she was pregnant, David made sure her husband, Uriah, was killed in battle (see 2 Samuel 11:1-27). We should never condone sin or overlook its repercussions, because God doesn't. He condemns sinful behavior, but when you truly repent as David did (Psalm 51), God will pick up where you derailed yourself and continue His sanctifying work. It's time to stop wallowing, get up, and cooperate with Him. Otherwise, you risk becoming barren and unfruitful (2 Peter 1:8).

BEARING HIS IMAGE BY INVESTING

Increasing in Christian graces is a sign of spiritual vigor, but I need to clarify that this has nothing to do with your personality. On the contrary, God made some people introverted, melancholy, and reserved—they're quiet listeners and observers. Others are extroverts—socializers who are comfortable front and center in a crowd, or as C.S. Lewis puts it, "being the big noise." But regardless of your personality, there should be excitement for God welling up inside you.

My home state of California is in constant motion. We don't always see or feel it, but with a phone app, you can connect to the United States Geological Survey (USGS) and follow the action. The USGS earthquake feed shows the measurable amount of daily ground movement—1.2, 3.7, 1.8, 4.0 on the Richter scale—all around the state. The movement we feel above ground is generated by the dynamic force of the Pacific and North American tectonic plates pushing past one another deep within the earth.

Similarly, our lives should show the presence of a deep source of energy. However, the danger for the believer isn't too much movement.

It's the lack of it. Peter described this in agricultural terms, "barren" and "unfruitful" (2 Peter 1:8).

The words "barren" and "unfruitful" are similar in meaning, and when you put them together, they create a disturbing word picture. Some Bibles translate the word "barren" as *idle*. The word *idle* fits with my geological illustration because it means inactive. "Barren" also means to be in a state of idleness, carelessness, or laziness, which describes what I call "flatline faith." When I hear the term *flatline*, I think of dead. But faith is a verb, so how can it be dead? Because it's not faith itself that qualifies its activity. It is the object that faith is placed in. Ouch!

Now, we're faced with a question: Is Jesus dead or alive? He is alive! My faith is in Him, who lives forevermore. Therefore, faith demands that I, Jack, be activated. Christ in my life should be consistently seen and felt. My life should have a sense of excitement and vitality, which raises another question: If I have faith in Him who is alive, how can I have a flatline faith? Ahh. Peter previously warned this would happen if we did not diligently grow in the Christian graces (2 Peter 1:8).

Barrenness regarding faith leads to a flatline faith that doesn't register on the scale, which is dangerous. And finding ourselves in a state of unfruitfulness isn't any better. To be unfruitful is to be unproductive and not invested. When it comes to faith, the more you invest, the better the results will be. I hope your thoughts didn't immediately go to money when I mentioned investing. Believers are called to invest themselves from the top of their heads to the soles of their feet to the glory of God.

Far too often, we play it safe spiritually because we don't want to look like a fool, or we're fearful of making a mistake. But when fear puts our faith into neutral and we sit idle, what we are doing is saying to God, "I doubt You. I know me, and You're probably not going to use me." Doubt puts the focus on self and eventually leads to a barren, unfruitful life. Don't do it! You will miss out.

The wise apostle Paul gently rebuked Timothy because Timothy was fearful; he was timid. Did Timothy miss wonderful adventures with the Lord because he gave in to his feelings? Probably. Which is why Paul reminded him, "God has not given us a spirit of fear, but of power and of love and of a sound mind" (2 Timothy 1:7). Do you and I need to hear that today? We do.

Young pastor Timothy was not alone in his hesitation. There was Moses, who God gave the mind-boggling assignment of leading the estimated two million unruly children of Israel out of the bondage of Egypt. Moses tried to tell God, "You can't use me. I stutter." God's reply? "Who has made man's mouth?" (Exodus 4:11). You can also add the prophet Jeremiah to the list of hesitators. God told Jeremiah, "Preach the truth to this nation." But Jeremiah protested, "I'm just a teenager. I can't do it" (see Jeremiah 1:6). God would not accept Jeremiah's disclaimer as an excuse. "But the LORD said to me: 'Do not say, "I am a youth," for you shall go to all to whom I send you, and whatever I command you, you shall speak. Do not be afraid of their faces, for I am with you to deliver you'" (Jeremiah 1:7-8). When God calls you to action, He knows all about your weaknesses and wants to use you anyway. It's my experience that the weaker, more tired, and spent I am, the more His power has been greater.

In the parable of the talents, Jesus addressed the issue of playing it safe (Matthew 25:14-30). He said, "The kingdom of heaven is like a man traveling to a far country, who called his own servants and delivered his goods to them. And to one he gave five talents, to another two, and to another one, to each according to his own ability."

The man gave his servants resources for use—three different allocations decided by the master. For the sake of clarity, we'll call them God-given opportunities. At this point, we often get tripped up for this reason: We don't trust our Master's judgment. We reason with ourselves that He has somehow made a mistake. But what Jesus is trying to convey is this: "When you're eager to do something for

My kingdom, that excitement comes from Me. And by the way, I've given you specific opportunities because I know the talents that I've given you—abilities you're probably not aware of, but I know you have them because I made you."

After the master gave his servants their allocations, he immediately left on a journey. Notice what they did with their God-given talents.

> He who had received the five talents went and traded with them, and made another five talents. And likewise he who had received two gained two more also. But he who had received one went and dug in the ground, and hid his lord's money. After a long time the lord of those servants came and settled accounts with them.
>
> So he who had received five talents came and brought five other talents, saying, "Lord, you delivered to me five talents; look, I have gained five more talents besides them." His lord said to him, "Well done, good and faithful servant; you were faithful over a few things, I will make you ruler over many things. Enter into the joy of your lord." He also who had received two talents came and said, "Lord, you delivered to me two talents; look, I have gained two more talents besides them." His lord said to him, "Well done, good and faithful servant; you have been faithful over a few things, I will make you ruler over many things. Enter into the joy of your lord" (Matthew 25:16-23).

Some scholars say, and I agree with them, that what is discussed here is that God gives every person the opportunity to live, at the very least. You are reading this, which means God has given you life. How are you investing it?

Keep in mind that the amount of the investment is determined by

God according to one's ability. In other words, stop looking at someone else's calling and ruling yourself out from investing in the kingdom because you can't do what they do! You are not supposed to do what they do. Take a deep breath and relax. God made you uniquely you, so it's foolish to compare yourself with others. "But they, measuring themselves by themselves, and comparing themselves among themselves, are not wise" (2 Corinthians 10:12). Let God be God in your life, and His sanctifying work will be turbocharged. His Word guarantees it.

Let God be God in your life, and His sanctifying work will be turbocharged. His Word guarantees it.

The parable ends with the wicked and lazy servant who, by his actions, revealed he was no servant of the master. He took the life his master gave, did nothing for his glory, and in the end, simply handed it back with no profit. And he received his just reward.

The Christian life is not in title and word only. It is a dynamic life full of excitement, passion, and growth. Jesus promised it. "On the last day, that great day of the feast, Jesus stood and cried out, saying, 'If anyone thirsts, let him come to Me and drink. He who believes in Me, as the Scripture has said, out of his heart will flow rivers of living water.' But this He spoke concerning the Spirit, whom those believing in Him would receive" (John 7:37-39).

The New King James phrase "cried out" sounds so gentle. Jesus screamed! Not only for all to hear, but for exaggerated emphasis of this truth: Out of the human heart believing in Me, life will flow. You would need to be Jewish to grasp the importance of this statement. Jews don't drink still, standing water because life-giving water is moving. Jesus was saying, "I'm the living water. If you associate with Me, living water will flow out of you too." But the qualifying factor is the Holy Spirit. We've already established that the Spirit indwells and seals every believer—that isn't what Jesus refers to here. He is talking about the Holy Spirit coming upon you for power and service. Christian graces will be witnessed through the power of the Spirit's outflow in your life.

As you turn the final page of this chapter, I hope it will be a turning point in your life. May you possess an intense passion for imitating Jesus until He comes again. Go forward in the Spirit's power and strength until you see your Lord face to face. Be bold and yield yourself to Christ!

CHAPTER 4

REMEMBER

Cross-country road trips are a fantastic way to experience the wonders of creation, not to mention mom-and-pop cafes and quirky roadside attractions. But before you can jump into your car and take off, you'll need an accurate map, a sound vehicle, a full gas tank, and a clear destination. In the same way, Bible-reading Christians know that some key essentials are required to navigate the ever-changing landscape of our world. Consulting the ultimate roadmap for life—the Bible, cooperating with the sanctifying work of the Holy Spirit, and keeping heaven in sight are at the top of the list. And it's always wise to listen and learn from seasoned travelers who have gone before you—men like Jude, Peter, and Paul. Consider these words from Jude:

> Beloved, while I was very diligent to write to you concerning our common salvation, I found it necessary to write to you exhorting you to contend earnestly for the faith...But I want to remind you, though you once knew this (Jude 1:3, 5).

You might be reading this and thinking, *I'm a believer. I know where I'm going and how to get there. I'm already on the road.* Great! You are precisely the person Jude was writing to. He knew how easily you can get comfortable in your Christianity and let the place where faith originated slip from memory. It's why God continually said, "Remember" to the children of Israel, and Jesus said, "Remember therefore" (Revelation 2:4-5) to those in the church at Ephesus, who had left their first love. Young believers and seasoned saints all need to have faith's fundamental truths repeatedly brought to the forefront of their minds.

FIGHT FOR YOUR FAITH

Jude was speaking to us, the church, in the last days when he wrote about our common salvation—how saved we are, and the power of God to keep us to the end. And he probably would have preferred to continue with that line of encouragement, but something more pressing was on his mind. Jude said, "Contend earnestly for the faith." Fighting for the faith is not the exclusive domain of pastors and ministries. It is God's mandate for the church as a whole and every Christian individually.

The call to contend for the faith requires the determination of wrestlers engaged in a match. Some believers are very uncomfortable with contending, others see it as optional, and today, still more question its necessity. Yet Scripture gives ample reasons to contend for our faith, with the primary one being false teaching. Jesus said many false prophets would arise before He returned (Matthew 24:11). Our English word translated as "arise" is an understatement. It makes the situation sound less critical than it is. The Greek translation says *not a few*, meaning a vast number of false teachers will permeate the landscape of the last days. It implies a coming drought of truth because of the false teachers and their doctrines that are on their way. I urge you to take a good look around. They are already here.

I have heard it said that the best defense against false teaching is true living. I say, "Amen" to that! A church filled with growing Christians, strong in faith, will not likely fall prey to counterfeit Christianity. But that presupposes that the Christians build their lives on the authoritative Word of God. Christians who rely on experience, at the expense of truth, find themselves in dangerous territory. False teachers cunningly target people who shun solid Bible learning in favor of experiences. And when you add the temptation of worldly alternatives, it's no wonder that Jude and other New Testament writers felt compelled to remind us of the essentials concerning our faith again and again and again. We need the reinforcement of biblical truth!

I want to reiterate that I am not condemning experiences—truth and experience are inseparable. Faith founded upon Christ and His Word ought to result in experiences, but depending on experiences to mold and shape our faith is wrong. Never allow experiences to dictate what you believe to be true because your experiences might not always align with the Bible. We should view experiences—the practical working out of God's Word—as exclamation points at the end of truth statements such as Isaiah 26:3, "You will keep him in perfect peace, whose mind is stayed on You because he trusts in You." I love that there exists an internal self-correcting feature built into the revelation of Scripture wherein the Bible judges all things, especially our experiences.

As tempting as it might be to scrutinize someone else's faith, we should examine ourselves by asking this essential question, "Is my faith grounded in biblical truth?"

YOUR FAITH IS IN CHRIST

Every person who teaches or speaks from our church pulpit stands on a bronze plaque embedded in the floor directly behind the podium. The plaque was installed on October 5, 2002, and it reads:

> Take care o' teacher that thou
> Giveth them Jesus!
> Thou who holdeth forth the Word of God,
> know that in this sanctuary, beneath thy feet,
> Lay the very Word of God—above which ye stand.
>
> These twenty four Bibles have gone out into the world
> and now have returned in this place.
>
> See to it then that the Lord speaketh unto thee out
> of it first before thou speaketh unto these His people,
> who art washed in His blood.
>
> Now then, if thou art certain of thy calling and if thou
> hast shown thyself approved unto God, and if thou
> hast prayed thyself ready, then let thyself go.
>
> For no other foundation can anyone lay than that
> which is laid, which is Jesus Christ.
>
> 1 Corinthians 3:11[1]

First Corinthians 3:11 was Paul's unrestrained, uncompromising apologetic. Is this the same confidence God wants you and me to have in our age? The answer is a resounding yes! The plaque serves as a reminder that the living Word of God, Jesus Christ, is the foundation of the New Testament church. Humanity cannot invent, create, or declare any other foundation that can withstand the test of time. Time always works for the benefit of the truth. In time, lies run out of gas and will be exposed while God's truth drives on.

Stay grounded in Christ and build upon His Word. Then, when someone says, "I need you to hear something, but you won't find it in the Bible—God gave it to me directly," a warning light will flash in your mind.

Faith that is acceptable to God is not founded upon anything new. He has not forgotten to tell us an essential piece of information that we need to know. There is no new truth waiting to be revealed, which is why Peter wrote to remind believers of their faith.

> For this reason I will not be negligent to remind you always of these things, though you know and are established in the present truth. Yes, I think it is right, as long as I am in this tent, to stir you up by reminding you knowing that shortly I must put off my tent, just as our Lord Jesus Christ showed me. Moreover I will be careful to ensure that you always have a reminder of these things after my decease (2 Peter 1:12-15).

Scholars believe that at the time Peter wrote this, he was in his late seventies and close to martyrdom. He was a wrinkled old man now, not the young man commissioned by Jesus to tend and feed His sheep (see John 21:16-17).

The idea of tending sheep must have sounded odd to a young fisherman with no sheep. But wooly animals weren't what Jesus had in mind. Jesus told Peter, "Instead of fish, you are going to scoop up the souls of Mister and Missus Mankind, whom I've called to be the sheep of My pasture. I want you to take good care of them and clean them up. Get the bugs and thorns out of their wool and the goop out of their eyes, but above all, make sure they are well fed" (see Jeremiah 3:15).

Decades passed, and Peter proved to be the kind of attentive pastor Jesus commissioned him to be. We know this because Peter said, "For this reason, I will not be negligent" (2 Peter 1:12). We would say it like this: "I'm not going to be careless or casual with what I'm about to say." Peter had learned difficult, hard-won lessons throughout years of ministry, but he will die soon, and he knows it. "Shortly,

I must put off my tent" was his way of saying, "I know I'm not long for this world." There is a sense of urgency and importance behind words like these, especially when they come from someone under a death sentence, as Peter was. A dying man has nothing to lose by telling the whole truth and nothing but the truth. And when a person has experienced the truth of God's Word as Peter did, we need to pay attention.

In the Greek language, the words translated "put off" means to put away, fold up, and break camp. When you are done camping and ready to go home, the last thing you do is fold up the tent. That is the same verbiage Peter used regarding his body. New tents are great. You buy one, take it to the campsite, and unfold it—boy, does it smell good. But by the time you've slept and sweated in that nylon enclosure for five, six, or seven years, you're ready to get rid of it. The zipper is broken and the roof leaks. Tents are useful, but they're temporary. Peter purposefully used this analogy to remind us about the brevity of our earthly lives.

Most of us don't have the luxury of knowing the time frame of our death, but in this respect, Peter had an advantage. Following Jesus' resurrection, Jesus told Peter he would die when he was old.

> "Most assuredly, I say to you, when you were younger, you girded yourself and walked where you wished; but when you are old, you will stretch out your hands, and another will gird you and carry you where you do not wish." This He spoke, signifying by what death he would glorify God. And when He had spoken this, He said to him, "Follow Me" (John 21:18-19).

Peter never forgot Jesus' words.

By focusing on his soon departure from this world, Peter was saying, "I won't be around much longer to give you guidance." Peter's point was that people come and go in our lives, but our faith transcends human dependence. God's Word endures but people don't. "The grass withers, the flower fades, but the word of our God stands forever" (Isaiah 40:8).

In times of trouble, our first reaction is often to go to a friend or relative, or even a pastor to give us answers. We put off praying. It's too hard, or it takes too long, and it requires discipline. Instead, we want someone to tell us what to do, and please do it quickly. I am grateful that the only pastor I've sat under, Chuck Smith, wouldn't do that. One day, I was in pastor Chuck's office asking for spiritual advice. He looked at me in a funny way, like I was an extraterrestrial, before gently pointing out, "The answer is in your Bible." He sat there with his big smile and said nothing else. I felt like I'd gotten spanked by the principal. But he was right.

Sometimes we need to seek wise counsel, but the Bible should always be the place we turn to first for guidance. It alone can do what another human cannot. "The word of God is living and powerful, and sharper than any two-edged sword, piercing even to the division of soul and spirit, and of joints and marrow, and is a discerner of the thoughts and intents of the heart" (Hebrews 4:12). We don't always need a person to provide us with answers, and that includes pastors. Our faith should stand firm upon Christ and His Word.

YOUR FAITH ISN'T IN A SYSTEM

The Bible, especially the book of Hebrews, makes it abundantly clear that our faith is not grounded in any man or system. In addition to Judaism, there are several religious systems people rely on, and not one will get them into heaven. Those systems will lead to God by way of judgment, but not an eternity with Him. Memberships won't do it either. Biblical saving faith has nothing to do with religiosity or church membership. Jesus told Nicodemus, a religious man, a Pharisee, and a ruler of the Jews, "Most assuredly, I say to you, unless one is born again, he cannot see the kingdom of God" (John 3:3). Yet countless times, I've been told, "I never heard that in my previous church." It's safe to say that before coming to Christ, many people were religionists who believed they were good enough. And if they failed at what they were endeavoring to do, they rolled up their sleeves, pulled up their bootstraps, and tried again, and again, and again.

A Jewish man once made an interesting comment that relates to who and what you're trusting in regarding faith. He said, "As a Jew, Jesus is okay. He was just nuts. It's Paul that we hate." Many in the Jewish community write Jesus off as being a lunatic, and I understand their thinking. Anybody who says, "I am the way, the truth, and the life. No one comes to the Father except through Me" (John 14:6) sounds loony—unless it's a documented historical fact that He was crucified, put in a tomb, and three days later, rose again. Paul, on the other hand, is a different story.

Many Jews hate Paul because he was one of them—until he became a turncoat and left Judaism behind to follow Jesus Christ. Paul knew the Old Testament scriptures better than most Jews, and when he said that he counted all his religious achievements as nothing (Philippians 3:7), we should listen and learn.

Religionists find the simple truth of the gospel offensive. But anything that causes you to lean on something or someone other than Jesus for salvation is a system or person that is anathema to God (see Galatians 1:6-9).

Years ago, I was asked to speak at one of the most gorgeous country clubs imaginable. I drove to an entrance with a sign that read "Members Only" and let the guard know I was there for the meeting. The guy gave me the "look" because I had no credentials, no golf clubs, and no proof that I belonged where I said I did. As he called whoever he needed to, in my mind, I imagined him saying, *We have a crazy here at the front gate wanting to get in.* Eventually, the guard returned and permitted me to enter, but before he did, he wanted me to know that he fully agreed with a particular theology, as if that were his ticket to heaven. But what if someone else says, "I'm a member of the Catholic, Greek Orthodox, or Baptist church"? If you are trusting in your religious affiliation or membership to secure your entrance into heaven, that, my friend, is unfortunate.

Some argue that church membership has benefits, but I ask, "For what purpose and for whom?" Is it to keep track of people, pay the bills, or have a vision for the next five months or five years? I've heard those reasons and more. I understand the desire for structure and hierarchy—we humans love schematics—but that isn't always the way God works. In his book *On Being a Servant of God*, Warren Wiersbe makes this point beautifully with a quote he attributes to Dr. Bob Cook: "If people can explain what is happening at your church, one thing is for sure. God is not the one doing it."[2]

Right in line with Dr. Wiersbe is the Biola University professor who told me, "The job that I do would cease to exist, and Bible colleges would be irrelevant, if churches would get off their southern section and do their first-century job of teaching the saints the Word of God." I would add to his observation that congregants need to ask themselves, "What would God have me to do with His Word?"

I know a man who spends Saturdays at the Huntington Beach Pier in Southern California. I adore him and love watching him in action. I've never seen anybody like him when it comes to the boldness that flows from genuine concern for the souls of men. He walks up to strangers and talks to them about eternity in a style straight out of heaven—winsome, loving, but to the point. Some couldn't care less, and they keep on walking. Others stop and listen. They may not like what they hear, but they can't deny it. This gentleman tells them that all of humanity is terminally ill—they are SIN positive—but there is a remedy, a cure. The Holy Spirit takes it from there, and he gives the gospel. Many are saved on the spot, while some say they'll think about it. My point is this: My friend is doing what God called him to do and is eternally impacting lives every time he does. He doesn't need a system to engage the culture. Neither do we.

If confronting a passerby about the reality of death seems morbid, it isn't. We'll all die at a time known only to God. John Wesley, the great preacher of yesteryear, is commonly credited with saying, "Until my work on this earth is done, I am immortal. But when my work for Christ is done…I go to be with Jesus." Wesley's statement is not the opinion of a spiritual madman. For the believer, it is a doctrinal fact. Until our appointed day, we are invincible in Christ! And the prospect of heaven should excite us to scoop up as many men, women, boys, and girls as we can and take them with us. Let's not hesitate to engage them with the facts they need to hear!

YOUR FAITH IS PRACTICAL

In the biblical sense, faith moves. Faith is active and moves us closer to God with every step it takes. Hebrews 10:38 says, "Now the just shall live by faith; but if anyone draws back, My soul has no pleasure in him." If I insert my name, the verse reads like this: "Now My righteous Jack shall live by faith; but if Jack draws back, My soul has no pleasure in him." Now you try it. Inserting your name makes the command to live by faith vault off the page!

This world's time clock is winding down. The hour has never been later, which is one more reason to drill down on the truth. Those with military backgrounds understand that drilling down means repeatedly doing the maneuver or exercise until it becomes second nature. Have you noticed how the Spirit does that in your private study of the Bible? How He faithfully brings you back around to what you already know to strengthen your understanding or mindset? For instance, you can read the book of Genesis ten different times, and each time, God will speak to you in another way. He will provide new insights just like He provided fresh manna for the children of Israel as they wandered in the wilderness. This also happens when you give eight pastors the same passage, and they teach eight different applications of the same truth. This is the Spirit's methodology—His way of repeatedly strengthening our resolve to allow faith to govern our lives entirely.

We can spiritualize our beliefs to the point where they have no practical value, but our conduct is where our beliefs are shown to be genuine or not. It isn't how much Bible we read in a day, but how much of it gets into us as a reality. Is there an adequate supply of scriptural doctrine in us to the point where it governs our lives? When you read warnings like 1 Corinthians 8:9, "Beware lest somehow this liberty of yours become a stumbling block to those who are weak," can you see potential applications? Let me illustrate what I mean by using examples about the way we dress and how we talk.

Most days, we get dressed and encounter the outside world. Men, many of you have built an impressive physique at the gym. You're proud of all that hard work and want to show it off with shirts that showcase your muscles. But to what end? Women, provocative styles garner attention, but what is your motivation? When you hear the Spirit of God say, "Maybe you shouldn't," then don't.

Perhaps your outward presentation is fine, but your heart isn't, and your words are the evidence. Now is the time to make a change.

> Whatever is in your heart determines what you say (Matthew 12:34 NLT).

> Don't use foul or abusive language. Let everything you say be good and helpful, so that your words will be an encouragement to those who hear them...Get rid of all bitterness, rage, anger, harsh words, and slander, as well as all types of evil behavior. Instead, be kind to each other,

tenderhearted, forgiving one another, just as God through Christ has forgiven you (Ephesians 4:29, 31-32 NLT).

Taking a bold stand isn't only about confronting enemies of the faith; it also means upholding righteousness in our personal lives. "The grace of God that brings salvation has appeared to all men, teaching us that, denying ungodliness and worldly lusts, we should live soberly, righteously, and godly in the present age" (Titus 2:11-12).

> Taking a bold stand isn't only about confronting enemies of the faith; it also means upholding righteousness in our personal lives.

RENEW FAITH'S PERSPECTIVE

The saints who have gone before us refused to accept a mediocre walk with Christ, and so must we. In the great hall of faith in Hebrews chapter 11, we read of faith lived out in Old Testament saints like Noah, Abraham, Sarah, Moses, Samuel, and David. Don't allow their stories to become so familiar that you forget the radicalness of what they did. For example, Noah built a giant boat at a time when rain was unheard of. Did others try to stop him, call him crazy, or worse? Most likely. Abraham and Sarah left all that was near and dear to them to follow God without a clear plan of where they were going. Were they scared and uncertain? Probably.

Think about it. The willingness of these Old Testament saints to put their faith to the test is an inspiration, yes, but also a challenge to us today.

In the New Testament, Paul's example of faith in action shows us a similar commitment. His conversion on the road to Damascus caused him to immediately ask, "Lord, what do You want me to do?" Paul's question should be the same one we ask every day. And then wherever God deploys you, be radical in that calling. I am not encouraging rude or offensive behavior. Being radical for Christ equates to living for Him, utterly and wholly, as we see Paul doing in Acts 20:18-21:

> You know, from the first day that I came to Asia, in what manner I always lived among you, serving the Lord with all humility, with many tears and trials which happened to me by the plotting of the Jews; how I kept back nothing that was helpful, but proclaimed it to you, and taught you publicly and from house to house, testifying to Jews, and also to Greeks, repentance toward God and faith toward our Lord Jesus Christ.

Paul was fulfilling Jesus' commissioning, but his ministry wasn't received with glorious fanfare. Acts 20:22-23 continues,

> Now I go bound in the spirit to Jerusalem, not knowing the things that will happen to me there, except that the Holy Spirit testifies in every city, saying that chains and tribulations await me.

I appreciate that the Bible never candy-coats the cost of following Christ. Bound in his spirit, Paul had to go. He could not do anything but go to Jerusalem, not knowing "the things that will happen to me there." Stop and put yourself in his sandals. Can you imagine what was going through Paul's mind? *I know God is sending me to Jerusalem. My heart is burning to preach the gospel to my people, and it's going to be painful, but I've got to go.* Yet Paul's perspective pushed him forward with joy.

> None of these things move me; nor do I count my life dear
> to myself, so that I may finish my race with joy, and the
> ministry which I received from the Lord Jesus, to testify
> to the gospel of the grace of God (verse 24).

When Paul set sail for Tyre, he was warned, "Paul, the Lord has shown us that you're going to be chained, arrested, and it isn't going to go well for you." Imagine if you were warned that you were going to be beaten and arrested for preaching Christ in Los Angeles, Detroit, or New York City. Would you still go? Despite the warnings, Paul continued.

> Then Paul answered, "What do you mean by weeping and
> breaking my heart? For I am ready not only to be bound,
> but also to die at Jerusalem for the name of the Lord Jesus."
> So when he would not be persuaded, we ceased, saying,
> "The will of the Lord be done" (Acts 21:13-14).

Why would someone answer God's call so boldly? What makes a person run headlong into insult and injury? It's just one thing: their love for their Savior eclipses the need for self-preservation.

Oh, how I wish all believers would get that under their skin. We all need passion—hot hearts—for God, that translates into determination, meaning, and purpose. Imagine if we found Jesus, stood for Jesus, and caught fire for Jesus. Only then would we be undeterred and unstoppable!

Are you young and looking for direction for your life? Follow Him. Middle-aged? Very old with little time remaining? Follow Him. The call upon every believer's life is to follow Jesus. Young or old, let's not waste one more minute by allowing opportunities to slip away.

If you find yourself distant from God, with all that's happening in our dark world, it is obvious that today is the day to recommit yourself to Jesus. Perhaps sin has obscured your way. Let me remind you that it has been said, "A journey of one thousand miles begins with the first step." God has been patiently waiting for you. It is time for you to say to Him, "I will arise and go to my father" (Luke 15:18) with the assurance that "if we confess our sins, He is faithful and just to forgive us our sins and to cleanse us from all unrighteousness" (1 John 1:9).

Now is the time to wisely number your days and redeem them for Christ, being careful that your earthly life reflects an eternal perspective (Psalm 90:12; Ephesians 5:16). I encourage you to get up every morning and say, "Lord Jesus, I don't know how many days I have left, but I want to use them well. I'm all in with whatever You have for me today. Holy Spirit, stir up my faith, shake out complacency, and provoke me to action!"

CHAPTER 5

BE CONFIDENT

Biblical faith has never been warm and fuzzy. It is unflinching and dynamic, able to take you through life and into the presence of Almighty God. I remind you of this because our culture's opposition to truth and acceptance of mistruths and outright lies is gaining speed. Yet, as God's people, our calling is to be like the sons of Issachar, who understood the times and seasons and knew what to do (1 Chronicles 12:32). We must stand as watchmen on the wall (Isaiah 62:6-7; Ezekiel 3:17-21), confidently speaking the truth. The good news is that faith in Jesus Christ creates a tremendous ability for believers to persevere and hold fast to their convictions.

CONFIDENT IN THE FACTS

In Proverbs 4:25, Solomon says, "Let your eyes look straight ahead, and your eyelids look right before you." In other words, don't let your eyes wander from the target. His highlighting of our *eyelids* is interesting. It means to look straight down to where your foot steps and where it will move next. Solomon then says, "Ponder the path of your feet, and let all your ways be established. Do not turn to the right or the left; remove your foot from evil" (verses 26-27). The only way to walk spiritually without turning to the left or right is to follow biblical truth. The problem today is that truth is under fire to the point of affecting people's choices and lifestyles.

In the not-so-distant past, there were two kinds of truth—objective truth based on facts, and subjective truth, or personal opinion. Today, we've entered a realm of non-thinking in which people say, "I don't care to think through a topic based on facts. I want to feel it." But the problem goes even further. Things once considered objective are now labeled subjective. It's become a case of my truth versus your truth. Propagating this kind of thinking are online dictionaries like Dictionary.com, where a search for the word *fact* leads to these definitions:

> **Fact**
> *noun*
>
> 1. that which actually exists or is the case; reality or truth: *Your fears have no basis in fact.*
>
> 2. something known to exist or to have happened: *Space travel is now a fact.*
>
> 3. a truth known by actual experience or observation; something known to be true: *Scientists gather facts about plant growth.*
>
> 4. something said to be true or supposed to have happened: *The facts given by the witness are highly questionable.*[1]

The first definition hits the mark, as does number two—something known to exist or have happened, such as space travel. Has space travel happened? Yes, it has. Number three defines a fact as a truth known by actual experience or observation, such as scientists gathering facts about plant growth. Again, I agree. Now take a careful look at definition four and its example. Number four completely contradicts the first three definitions! What started as declarations of facts being objective truth ends with facts being highly questionable because maybe they are true or maybe not. That is irrational! Facts are facts, and truth is truth, period. No wonder people are confused.

It is important to understand that the Bible's unchanging truth, as it is lived out individually, is also subjective because *how* it affects us is personal. You and I can agree that "He who has begun a good work in you will complete it" (Philippians 1:6) is a fact, knowing that how God chooses to complete the work in us will differ. Unlike questionable sources, God's objective and subjective truths—perfectly coupled—allow us to draw sound conclusions with confidence.

THE CONFIDENCE OF EYEWITNESSES

How trustworthy are the facts of our faith? The opening verses of the book of Acts tell us.

> The former account I made, O Theophilus, of all that Jesus began both to do and teach, until the day in which He was taken up, after He through the Holy Spirit had given commandments to the apostles whom He had chosen, to whom He also presented Himself alive after His suffering by many infallible proofs, being seen by them during forty days and speaking of the things pertaining to the kingdom of God (Acts1:1-3).

Luke reminds Theophilus that in his Gospel, he wrote about the amazing things that took place from the beginning of Jesus' ministry to His ascension into heaven. Luke continues his narrative in the book of Acts and uses two important phrases to emphasize the factual basis of both accounts—"many infallible proofs" and "being seen by them." The facts surrounding Jesus are corroborated by the people of His time.

Skeptics argue, "That's just what the Bible claims," and they are correct. It is. Yet the Bible is prepared to answer that criticism—when it makes a claim, eyewitnesses and the unbelieving world are involved. Jesus didn't teach and work miracles in a back alley or hidden corner. He did His Father's work in front of friends and foes alike under the watchful eyes of the Roman Empire.

I thank God that we have eyewitness accounts to verify the reality of our faith. Regarding what John witnessed, he wrote,

> That which was from the beginning, which we have heard, which we have seen with our eyes, which we have looked upon, and our hands have handled, concerning the Word of life—the life was manifested, and we have seen, and bear witness, and declare to you that eternal life which was with the Father and was manifested to us (1 John 1:1-2).
>
> The Word became flesh and dwelt among us, and we beheld His glory, the glory as of the only begotten of the Father, full of grace and truth (John 1:14).

Peter also wrote about being an eyewitness of Christ's majesty. "We did not follow cunningly devised fables when we made known to you the power and coming of our Lord Jesus Christ, but were eyewitnesses of His majesty" (2 Peter 1:16).

Seeing Transformation

The power and majesty that Peter is referring to is what he, James, and John witnessed on the Mount of Transfiguration:

> Now after six days Jesus took Peter, James, and John his brother, led them up on a high mountain by themselves; and He was transfigured before them...Suddenly a voice came out of the cloud, saying, "This is My beloved Son, in whom I am well pleased. Hear Him!" And when the disciples heard it, they fell on their faces and were greatly afraid (Matthew 17:1-2, 5-6).

Keep in mind that every ancient culture had its deities and stories, including those of the Greco-Roman Empire, but Peter said that Jesus' transfiguration wasn't a fable. The Greek translation of "cunningly devised fables" means "well-crafted myths." Myths are stories of men and women imaginatively mixed with fantastic writing and pseudo-insights that stimulate and captivate—like *Lord of the Rings* or the *Harry Potter* series. But Peter, James, and John didn't fabricate an enticing tale to incite others to follow Jesus. Nor did the guys get together and say, "Let's invent a story, market it, and see what we can get out of it." John and Peter simply recorded what they witnessed.

The Bible says, "By the mouth of two or three witnesses every word shall be established" (2 Corinthians 13:1). The claim of the transfiguration involves the sworn testimony of three eyewitnesses and historical documents that are still in existence. If this event were brought into a courtroom, the biblical accounts of the transfiguration would be admissible evidence, so it is important to understand what took place.

Peter said that he and others witnessed the majesty of Christ. Matthew tells us that it took place when Jesus took Peter, James, and John and scaled a high mountain. In theology, the word *when* in Matthew 17:6 is known as a time stamp that indicates something real, something tangible took place. Peter's testimony under oath might have gone something like this: "The three of us saw Jesus praying. We were a stone's throw away from Him and, as we watched, He was transfigured right in front of us. He began to shine brighter than the sun! The sky dimmed at the brilliance of Jesus. It was amazing! We saw explosive, dynamic, unnatural power—the power of God's kingdom! I saw it, James saw it, and John saw it too. We were all eyewitnesses."

The babe born in Bethlehem was God veiled in human skin with all His glory concealed inside. But on the mount, when Jesus began to pray, His Spirit, in communion with the Father, allowed the glory inside Him to be revealed. I wonder if Jesus' human skin appeared to wither as the eternal glory of Christ emanated outward. What we do know is that His face shone as the sun, His clothes were brighter than light itself, and Moses and Elijah appeared with Jesus, talking with Him (Matthew 17:3), until

> a bright cloud overshadowed them; and suddenly a voice came out of the cloud, saying, "This is My beloved Son, in whom I am well pleased. Hear Him!" And when the disciples heard it, they fell on their faces and were greatly afraid. But Jesus came and touched them and said, "Arise, and do not be afraid." When they had lifted up their eyes, they saw no one but Jesus only (verses 5-7).

The mountain was quiet, the moment was over, and the three opened their eyes to the familiar figure of Jesus standing alone; Moses and Elijah were gone. Ask any Jew, and they will tell you that Moses represents the law and Elijah the prophets—the power these men witnessed transcended both. They could never go back to following any system or person, only Jesus. Peter, James, and John tasted the glory and power of heaven, and they had no appetite for anything else. No wonder you couldn't keep these men from spreading the gospel!

Seeing Power

Humanity trends toward an obsession with power. Yet the greatest power in the world pales in comparison to Jesus Christ—the power of the kingdom—coming from heaven to dwell among men.

Years ago, at a crusade in Tampa, Florida, a man interrupted Billy Graham's message with, "If God is God, I'm gonna give him one minute and let him strike me dead." Nothing happened. An elderly man in the front row said, "My friend, you cannot exhaust the patience of God in one minute."[2] In saying this, the man was giving witness to the fact that God's power was displayed by His patience. Similarly, the Bible says that Jesus' power was restrained by His *meekness*, which some might equate with weakness. But the biblical definition of *meekness* is power under control.

Remember how the Roman soldiers mocked Jesus, saying, "If you are the King of the Jews, save Yourself" (Luke 22:37)? Or when He was blindfolded and struck on the face (Luke 22:63-64)? In both instances, Jesus could have turned His tormentors into dust, but He didn't. Why? Hebrews 12:2 says, "Jesus, the author and finisher of our faith, who for the joy that was set before Him endured the cross, despising the shame." Jesus had a date with the cross.

Years later, when Peter wrote about the transfiguration, he said, "He received from God the Father honor and glory when such a voice came to Him from the Excellent Glory: 'This is My beloved Son, in whom I am well pleased'" (2 Peter 1:17). The voice heard on the mount came from the Excellent Glory, translated *doxa* in the Greek language. We read about the all-surpassing brilliance of God's majesty, or *doxa*, in various places in the Bible, including passages that reveal that the same glory and nature is in Jesus Christ.

> Jesus came and spoke to them, saying, "All authority has been given to Me in heaven and on earth" (Matthew 28:18).

He is the image of the invisible God, the firstborn over all creation. For by Him all things were created that are in heaven and that are on earth, visible and invisible, whether thrones or dominions or principalities or powers. All things were created through Him and for Him. And He is before all things, and in Him all things consist. And He is the head of the body, the church, who is the beginning, the firstborn from the dead, that in all things He may have the preeminence. For it pleased the Father that in Him all the fullness should dwell (Colossians 1:15-19).

Now may the God of peace who brought up our Lord Jesus from the dead, that great Shepherd of the sheep, through the blood of the everlasting covenant, make you complete in every good work to do His will, working in you what is well pleasing in His sight, through Jesus Christ, to whom be glory forever and ever. Amen (Hebrews 13:20-21).

When I saw Him, I fell at His feet as dead. But He laid His right hand on me, saying to me, "Do not be afraid; I am the First and the Last. I am He who lives, and was dead, and behold, I am alive forevermore. Amen. And I have the keys of Hades and of Death" (Revelation 1:17-18).

The Excellent Glory was of both God and the Savior, and the world will see His glory again!

Immediately after the tribulation of those days the sun will be darkened, and the moon will not give its light; the stars will fall from heaven, and the powers of the heavens will be shaken. Then the sign of the Son of Man will appear in heaven, and then all the tribes of the earth will mourn, and they will see the Son of Man coming on the clouds of heaven with power and great glory (Matthew 24:29-30).

Do you see why the Lord Jesus Christ is worthy of your worship and adoration and why you can confidently follow Him every moment of every day?

I appreciate how the Bible unapologetically lays out the facts for us to decide whether it is true or not. No one trusts a person whose story is constantly changing, and if Christianity is not founded on true eyewitness accounts, how do you explain the willingness of the disciples to follow Jesus unto death?

We are told that Andrew, Philip, Simon, Peter, and Bartholomew were all crucified for their faith. Peter was crucified upside down, and Bartholomew was nearly beaten to death before his crucifixion. If their faith rested on make-believe stories, don't you think they would have given up and saved themselves the horror of such brutal deaths? And then there was James, the son of Alphaeus, Judas, also called Thaddeus, and Matthias, who were stoned to death. James, the son of Zebedee, was beheaded, and Thomas was gored to death. John was the only disciple who died of natural causes. He was exiled to the barren rocky island of Patmos, but church history suggests this was only after he miraculously survived being boiled in oil! He could have decided enough was enough, but God gave him the book of Revelation instead (Revelation 1:10).

The driving force in the disciples' lives was Jesus Christ. They were willing to die for what they knew to be true of Him, and they weren't alone. Countless others, known and unknown, throughout the ages have willingly laid down their lives for the gospel. I don't want to belabor the point, but you should never believe something without knowing the factual evidence behind your faith. But once you know the facts, what will you do with them? Contained inside our bodies is the treasure of the gospel, the greatest message in all the world. So let's stop playing it safe. It's time to be confident and courageous!

THE CONFIDENCE OF INFALLIBLE PROOF

It's human nature to want to see power or a miracle before we believe. But better than power or a miracle, we have "a more sure word of prophecy" (2 Peter 1:19 KJV). If Peter were here today, he would say, "In light of everything I've seen and observed, the Bible is surer because His Word is the final authoritative word."

> Contained inside our bodies is the treasure of the gospel, the greatest message in all the world. So let's stop playing it safe. It's time to be confident and courageous!

When the Bible says it is a "more sure word of prophecy," it means that God's Word has gone ahead of you. God has a plan, and He's announced it in advance. The New Living Translation did a good job with this verse: "Because of that experience [the transfiguration], we have even greater confidence in the message proclaimed by the prophets" (2 Peter 1:19). Oh, how many of us need to hear this today! We tiptoe around our faith in front of others. Why do we suffer angst, anguish, worry, and fear when God's promises are ours to take hold of? Why do we act as if He is a liar? We would never say such a thing out loud, but when we don't believe what God says, it is tantamount to the same as calling Him a liar.

A proper understanding of God's prophetic Word places the Christian in the immediate now of ministry. Christians with a correct view of what the Bible says about the future are…

1. *Watchmen.* God has given all believers eyes to see and ears to hear (Matthew 13:16), but watchmen are committed to keeping an eye on the culture and sounding the alarm when needed.

2. *Evangelistic.* Every soul is precious, and no one is beyond God's ability to save. Oh, that we would set aside fear and timidity to reach others with the gospel of Jesus Christ! "How beautiful...are the feet of him who brings good news, who proclaims peace, who brings glad tidings of good things, who proclaims salvation" (Isaiah 52:7).

3. *Understanding.* When it comes to unsaved friends and family, it feels like time is against us because it is running out, but it also works for us by creating a sense of urgency. The world is ripe for judgment, and Christ can return anytime. So we should be eager to share the gospel. Yet we can relax. God knows exactly the right moment for you, me, and our loved ones to enter eternity through either the rapture or breathing our last.

The surety of the eyewitnesses combined with prophecy should serve to increase our confidence!

I think everyone, Christian or not, can agree that the Bible is an amazing book. Yet some will say, "I don't believe the Bible. But more to the point, I don't see why I should care." Well, to not believe the Bible is a matter of choice. It is subjective. But what if there is some possibility that it is correct, and heaven and hell are both very real? Then what? Can a person be absolutely sure the Bible is wrong? Because if the person is wrong and the Bible is right, there is a lot at stake.

Believing the Bible doesn't require a leap of faith or leaving your brain behind, as some have alleged. We've seen that eyewitnesses of

Jesus' life never changed their story, so we know we can trust their testimony.

Acts 1:3 states that the life and ministry of Jesus was confirmed by "many infallible proofs" in relation to the events that followed Jesus' resurrection. Christ's resurrection testifies to the power of God (Ephesians 1:19-20), was verified by hundreds of witnesses (1 Corinthians 15:6), and is irrefutable proof that He is the promised Savior.

We use two English words, "infallible proofs," to describe a single word in the original Greek language, *tekmerion*, meaning a mark, a sign, a convincing proof, or evidence. While you don't need to defend the Bible because it speaks for itself, you should know the facts concerning God's Word. There are many criteria for judging the accuracy and trustworthiness of God's Word. Let's look at a few, beginning with what the Bible is.

PUT IT TO THE TEST

The word *Bible* comes from the Latin word *biblia*, which means the books or collection of books. The Bible is divided into two parts: the Old Testament, which explains history before the time of Jesus Christ, and the New Testament, which explains history during and immediately after the time of Christ. This leads to why it is reliable.

The Bible comprises 66 books written by 40 different writers over a span of 1,500 years. One of the features that makes it unique is the perfect harmony of the entire book. Historically, archaeologically, and scientifically accurate, it is without error or contradiction in its original Hebrew, Greek, and Aramaic manuscripts. Each of the 66 books complements, corroborates, and works toward one mighty crescendo—Jesus Christ—with one ultimate author. "All Scripture is given by inspiration of God, and is profitable for doctrine, for reproof, for correction, for instruction in righteousness" (2 Timothy 3:16).

Test upon Test: The Honesty Test

Jesus regularly quoted from the Old Testament books of Genesis, Exodus, Leviticus, Deuteronomy, Psalms, Proverbs, Isaiah, Jeremiah, Ezekiel, Daniel, Hosea, Amos, Jonah, Micah, and Malachi—therefore validating what the authors wrote. In the New Testament, the Gospel writers Matthew, Mark, Luke, and John all presented themselves as eyewitnesses recording history. Because the New Testament authors claim to speak the truth regarding Jesus, let's give them the honesty test. Did they also include embarrassing material about themselves?

The significance behind including not-so-nice details means they were more concerned about recording the truth than preserving their reputation. In other words, if they wanted to lie about events, why not do it in a way that made them look good? Does the Bible record awkward information about its writers? Yes, it does.

- Jesus called Peter Satan—not a good name to be called (Matthew 16:23).

- James and John had their mother ask Jesus to give them places of honor in His kingdom (Matthew 20:21).

- In the Garden of Gethsemane, knowing that His arrest was imminent, Jesus told His disciples to pray before leaving to pray by Himself. Jesus returned not once or twice, but three times to find them all sleeping (Mark 14:37, 40, 41).

- When the Roman soldiers arrested Jesus, the disciples bolted. They ditched their best friend in a heartbeat (Matthew 26:56).

- While Jesus was questioned, spat on, and struck, Peter sat in the courtyard warming himself. When asked about Jesus, Peter denied Him three times, while the other disciples were hiding somewhere (Matthew 26:69-75).

What do details like these tell us? The authors believed it was their duty to give the whole truth. I gave you a few examples from the Gospels, but there are also plenty of humiliating accounts recorded in the Old Testament.

Test upon Test: The Telephone Test

Next, how do we know that the Bible isn't like the children's game of Telephone? This game begins with one person whispering a message into the ear of another person, who then relays it to the next. This continues until the message reaches the last person in the group, who repeats the message out loud. Almost without fail, the final message comes out as a convoluted version of the original, making everyone laugh. While testing the integrity of the Bible isn't a game, we can apply the Telephone game "test" to see if the contents of the original documents have reached our modern-day Bibles accurately.

This test requires us to know the gap of time from the original manuscripts to the first existing copies we have in hand. The smaller the gap, the less room there is for error and the more reliable the copy is. There are ancient documents other than the Bible that help us get a better understanding of how the Bible measures up from an accuracy standpoint.

Pliny the Younger was a Roman historian. The time gap between his original manuscripts and the existing copies is 750 years. Caesar's firsthand account of the Gallic Wars has a time gap of 1,000 years between the original manuscripts and the copies. Plato's *Tetrologies* has a gap of 1,200 years. In contrast, the time gap for the New Testament is a mere 50 years! We have New Testament copies of the Scriptures that were written within 50 years of Jesus' lifetime. Allow those differences to sink in for a moment.

The first biography we have of Alexander the Great was written 400 years after he lived, and no one questions who he was and what he did. Yet we have *four* biographies of Jesus—the Gospels—written within 50 years of His lifetime, and yet people still want to dispute His words and deeds. In fact, the evidence supporting Jesus' life easily outweighs the evidence for all the other ancient figures in history. If we're not willing to trust the records about Jesus, then logically, we cannot trust what we think or know about other persons or accounts of ancient history.

Test upon Test: The Number of Copies Extant Test

What about the total number of copies in existence? Does that matter? Yes, it does. More copies equal more evidence and a better chance that the copies were faithful to the original. The account that we have about Caesar, a contemporary of Jesus, has ten copies in existence. Plato's *Tetralogies* and Pliny's letters have only seven copies each.

What about copies of the Greek New Testament? If you said 5,600 and counting, you are right. In addition, there are more than 19,000 copies of the New Testament in the Syriac, Latin, Coptic, and Aramaic languages. The total supporting New Testament manuscript base is more than 24,600!

Now, guess which historical manuscript is next in line for the most copies extant? It's Homer's *Iliad*, with about 643. Please permit me to indulge in a bit of sarcasm with my next statement: Homer's second-place award trails the New Testament by a mere 23,957 copies. The evidence for the accuracy of our Bibles is overwhelming! Again, I urge you to take a moment to process the facts.

Test upon Test: The Corroboration Test

Now that we've covered the honesty, Telephone game, and extant copies tests, let's apply the corroboration test. This asks the question, Do other historical materials confirm or deny the testimony of the Bible? There are nine non-Christian sources that mention Jesus within 150 years of His death, plus another 33 Christian sources. Together, that's 42 sources other than the Bible that speak about Jesus. Caesar has ten sources that mention him within 150 years of his death. Jesus has four times as many historical references. So even if we *exclude* the Bible, we can know from other sources that Jesus lived, did miracles, had people believe in Him, was worshipped as God, was crucified, died, was buried, rose from the grave on the third day, appeared to His disciples and others, and ascended into heaven, but not before promising He would one day come again. That, my friend, should challenge you to follow Jesus with all confidence!

MOVE FORWARD WITH CONFIDENCE

All manner of tests can be done to prove the reliability of God's Word, but the one skeptics tend to overlook is, What effect does the Bible have on those who believe it and live by it? Oxford professor of mathematics John Lennox gives ample factual evidence for the reliability of the Bible in his book *Can Science Explain Everything?* But in the final chapter he writes, "Christianity is also eminently testable at the personal level," and he shares a story that points to perhaps the greatest evidence of all—a changed life.

> Some time ago I was lecturing in a major US university, speaking about the credibility of Christianity. Immediately after I had finished up, up in the balcony, a Chinese student stood up and loudly cried, "Look at me!" It was quite startling and we all looked. I addressed him and said, "Why should we look at you?" His reply went something like this: "Six months ago my life was in a mess: I had no peace and I saw no way out. I was taken to a lecture you gave in another university, and something you said triggered a response in me. A few weeks later I gave my life to Christ. Just look at me now!" He was radiating a joy that all of us could see. He had tested Christianity and found it to be true.[3]

Many people claim that the Bible is a book of myths that cannot be trusted, despite the verification of infallible proofs, eyewitness evidence, and personal experiences. The reliability, strength, and veracity of the enduring Word of God is indisputable. Skeptics and enemies try to scale Scripture's walls and break down its defenses, yet whenever the Bible is challenged and tested, it stands strong, and so should we.

The wonder of God's Word is that it is constantly speaking, always illuminating, and forever showing us the way to go. But whenever we come to a fork in the road, we are faced with one of two ways—doubt or belief, with one canceling the other. To doubt is to dismiss, which leaves you vulnerable and without hope. But to believe and obey is to live and act and speak freely with courage.

God stands before us in His Word, asking you and me to look to Him and trust Him. He is beckoning us to move forward in faith and refuse to sit as idle spectators of what He wants to accomplish in these last days. You might be thinking, *What if I act on what I know to be true, and nothing happens?* My answer is this: You will have done your best for the glory of God, and that, dear saint, is what matters most. Let what you perceive as failure rest in His hands, confident that the Lord's will was done through you.

I liken what you have read thus far to a spiritual boot camp—basic training, if you will—designed to strengthen and encourage your inner man in preparation to face the enemies of your soul. Now that you know who you are and what is yours in Christ Jesus, some reconnaissance is in order. It is time to examine the strategic features of who you are up against.

PART 2
WATCH OUT

CHAPTER 6

WATCH AND LISTEN

✝

Bible-believing Christians have a unique view of life—we look to the future with excitement and in anticipation of heaven, yet we reside in the present. Which one should we live for? Both, of course! And because God has not yet taken us home, we have a mission to complete. Every Christian has been enlisted to fight in a spiritual war that began in the Garden of Eden—the battle against darkness and evil. Paul told Timothy, "You therefore must endure hardship as a good soldier of Jesus Christ" (2 Timothy 2:3). You aren't likely to find that on a Bible promise card, yet it's true.

A soldier's life differs from a civilian's life in many ways. Soldiers set aside the comforts of their pre-enlistment life to dedicate themselves to pleasing their commanding officer. "No one engaged in warfare entangles himself with the affairs of this life, that he may please him who enlisted him as a soldier" (2 Timothy 2:4). And soldiers also train themselves to carefully watch for enemy movements by keeping their eyes and ears open and attentive. In the lexicon of the Marine Corps Combat Hunter program, this is called being "left of bang." This training enables soldiers to detect an enemy's evil intentions before they happen. Being left of bang works like this:

If you were to think about an attack on a timeline, bang is in the middle. Bang is the act. Bang is the IED explosion, the sniper taking a shot, or the beginning of an ambush. Bang is what we want to prevent. Being left of bang means that a person has observed one of the pre-event indicators, one of the warning signs, that must occur earlier on the timeline for the bang to happen. Being left of bang means not letting the insurgent carry through with the plan to kill American troops. Being on the other end of the timeline is referred to as being "right of bang." Whenever a person is operating right of bang, it means that the enemy has the initiative and controls the situation.[1]

Well-trained soldiers not only understand their environment and its dynamics, they also intend to win. Ancient Chinese warrior Sun Tzu put it like this: "Victorious warriors win first and then go to war, while defeated warriors go to war first and then seek to win." Did you know Jesus made that same point? He said nobody goes into battle until they first figure out that they've got the wherewithal to not only engage in a war, but to also finish it. "What king, going to make war against another king, does not sit down first and consider whether he is able with ten thousand to meet him who comes against him with twenty thousand?" (Luke 14:31). Christian, behind you are all the resources of heaven. You have what it takes!

The same dynamics of a soldier's life constitute the call and challenge for believers today because the church—perhaps your church—is in great peril. The danger isn't coming from outside, but within.

That might sound like hyperbole, but others agree. Pastor and theologian Mark Hitchcock said, "The greatest danger to the church today is not humanism, paganism, atheism, or agnosticism. The greatest danger is not increasing hostility against our faith from the culture. Our greatest danger is apostasy on the inside arising from false teachers, theological liberals who deny and distort biblical doctrine and lead others down the same path."[2]

Wherever God is moving, your enemy, the devil, will infiltrate. Bank on it. He does not care about a sleepy church that is powerless and ineffective. In fact, a carnal and lethargic church is a good tool in his hands. Satan leaves that church alone. He won't tamper with it. But wherever God is using His people to change lives, you can expect demonic trouble.

FALSE TEACHERS ABOUND

Watch Out for Wolves

False teachers are nothing new. They were among the Jewish people throughout Israel's existence in biblical times and are among Christians in the church today. Peter warned, "There were also false prophets among the people, even as there will be false teachers among you" (2 Peter 2:1).

Peter's warning "there will be" is a strong one. Wherever people who love Jesus are gathered with Bibles open, you can count on false teachers trying to move in. It's a strange promise, but one I'm grateful for. This keeps us on our toes because these teachers aren't run-of-the-mill cult adherents. They are in our midst, which is why Paul also warned, "I know this, that after my departure savage wolves will come in among you, not sparing the flock" (Acts 20:28-29).

The imagery of false teachers as wolves is both alarming and horrible—with their deadpan faces they seem cold, calculated, and emotionless. Wolves hide by blending into the background as they follow elk or caribou herds for days, waiting for an elk or a caribou to lag behind. Maybe it's a tired old male or an unsuspecting calf. It doesn't matter to the wolf. The wolf will hang its head, very coy-like, as if to say, "Don't worry, I'm not a threat to you." It will creep closer and closer until it's within striking range, and then it will attack.

Sometimes, a wolf will bring down an animal by strategic nipping. Other times, it will lunge for the throat and hang on until the rest of the pack comes in for the kill. This is the picture that the apostle Paul wants believers to see in their mind's eye because in the spiritual realm, these are the tactics of false teachers.

The longest-running attack by Satan and his cohorts is against God's word, beginning with His spoken word to Eve and later His written Word. Satan will do everything possible to pollute, dilute, misrepresent, and change it. The Bible you read today is the same one written more than 21 centuries ago. We know this because from 1947 to 1956, ancient Old Testament manuscripts, the Dead Sea Scrolls, were recovered from clay jars hidden in Judaean caves at Qumran, an archeological site I have visited many times over the years. And more recently, Israeli archaeologists announced the discovery of additional fragments in March 2021.

When you compare the Old Testament in your Bible with ancient manuscripts and fragments, you'll discover they say the same thing, almost verbatim. Why is this important? All the prophecies and events during Old Testament times point to God's eternal plan of salvation, which we read about in the New Testament. Together, the Old and New Testaments comprise one seamless, cohesive book.

Satan attacks the Bible because, when rightly given, it will bear fruit throughout the world (Colossians 1:5-6). On October 7, 2023, the terrorist organization Hamas executed an unimaginably barbaric attack on Israel, resulting in war. God may not have caused it, but He used that dark time, and remarkable fruit was born. Jews began asking questions and seeking answers from the Old Testament scriptures, with some realizing that Yeshua (Jesus) is Messiah, and accepting Him as their Lord and Savior. Satan hates it when "the lost sheep of Israel" are plucked from his kingdom! He will pull out all the stops to keep anyone, Jew or Gentile, from the truth and out of heaven. This is why it's imperative for believers to watch out for wolves who seek to subvert the Bible.

Watch Out for Counterfeits

Your pastor's teaching may be doctrinally sound, but he has your attention only once, maybe twice, a week. Yet you live in a world of 24-hour, seven-days-a-week bombardment of spiritual programming on radio, television, and the internet. Watch out! What you hear and read might sound right on, but false teachers' words are perverse (Acts 20:29). By that I don't mean they swear. Rather, what they say is spiritually corrupt and doctrinally incorrect and demonically empowered.

How can you know whether a message falls into the category of perverse? It is impossible to know everything about all the religions, cults, and teachers that exist, but you can discern truth from lies by applying 1 Thessalonians 5:21: "Test all things." In biblical times, testing something meant holding it up to the light; you determined authenticity through careful scrutiny. Today, merchants do this with $50 and $100 bills. They hold a bill up to the light to see if the markings that declare the bill authentic are embedded in the paper.

We are called to test or scrutinize "all things," as in all kinds of things, including people, possibilities, situations, and angles. We are to be careful about everything in life.

Scrutinizing from all angles reminds me of an Israeli friend whose father read the Scriptures with his kids while they sat around the table. When it was their turn, the kids had to read aloud. But there was a catch: Dad never moved the Bible. Each child had to read it from where they were sitting. Some read upside down. Others had to turn their head or move their eyes or both. I asked, "Why did your dad do that?" My friend said, "From our earliest ages, our dad taught us to recognize God's truth from every angle." I like that!

In Amos 7:7, we read about Amos's vision of the Lord standing with a plumb line in His hand. Carpenters and do-it-yourselfers use plumb lines to test a wall's vertical trueness. Christian, your plumb line for sound doctrine is the Bible. Study it, and you will know whether what you are hearing is off-center or right on.

Don't let yourself get caught up in the charisma of teachers, no matter how appealing. Their true identity has nothing to do with how they present themselves. Rather, it has everything to do with how they live. Lifestyles matter. Equally important are their words because what comes out reveals the spirit embedded within. Is it the Spirit of truth, or a spirit of error?

Scripture tell us how to identify whether a spirit is of God. "By this you know the Spirit of God: Every spirit that confesses that Jesus Christ has come in the flesh is of God, and every spirit that does not confess that Jesus Christ has come in the flesh is not of God. And this is the spirit of the Antichrist, which you have heard was coming, and is now already in the world" (1 John 4:2-3). Cult followers and false believers often use the same words or phrases as we do, but their version of Jesus and way of salvation are in opposition to biblical truth.

People knocking on your door can agree that Jesus came in the flesh. Pastors can teach messages from a Bible in their pulpit. Yet if anyone tells you that keeping rules and regulations is necessary for salvation, they know nothing of His saving grace.

Salvation is all of Christ and all of grace, but grace is an affront to the intellectual pride of false teachers. They replace grace with the law, yet Galatians 3:24-25 says, "The law was our tutor to bring us to Christ, that we might be justified by faith. But after faith has come, we are no longer under a tutor." The law serves to remind us of the depth of our unrighteousness and our need for the one and only Savior (Romans 3:23). A true born-again believer gladly embraces salvation by grace alone because once Christ begins transforming us, we quickly learn it isn't easy to follow Him. But hallelujah! God's grace is there again, again, and again.

Watch Out for Believable Lies

False ministries secretly bring in "destructive heresies" (2 Peter 2:1). The King James Version calls such teachings "damnable heresies." Does damnable sound too harsh? It is not! False teachers subtly sneak in doctrines that condemn their followers to die without Christ. Bible commentator Albert Barnes's old English comment is eye-opening: "They come under plausible arts and pretenses."[3] In other words, they fabricate believable lies.

You cannot listen to false teaching week after week without your faith being affected because "a little leaven leavens the whole lump" (Galatians 5:9). I know a man who was active in ministry but was persuaded that he needed a Doctor of Divinity degree and enrolled in a Christian university. One of his professors opened the first day of class by boasting, "I have multiple degrees in history and antiquities. I am not a Christian, and I don't care to be a Christian. So don't try to convert me." It defies explanation as to why an unbeliever was teaching at a Christian college, but there he was.

The man thought, *Well, okay, thanks for the disclaimer*. Time went by, and eventually, his professor's worldview affected him. The professor's authority and purported wisdom, insight, and knowledge were so persuasive that he ended up changing some of the man's biblical views—key views, I might add.

Be careful who you expose yourself to. When I hear people confess, "I know this person is somewhat off, but I find them interesting," I say, "Stop listening!" False teachers can gather the masses by giving them unbiblical, ungodly, feel-good, warm-your-heart, make-you-happy heresy. Satan loves to traffic in those kinds of messages. If you question whether false teachers know they are wrong, the answer is yes. That line of questioning inevitably leads to, "Where does that put me if I'm saying things that aren't quite right? Am I a false teacher or prophet?" Not necessarily. Maybe you haven't read that part of the Bible yet, or the Holy Spirit is still helping you understand why a long-held belief is not scriptural, but you are learning and growing.

What if you have doubts? Doubt is native to us all. Doubt should drive us to the Bible to get answers because we fear being on the wrong side of what is true. If you are uncertain about anything regarding Jesus Christ or your faith, it's okay. Go search God's Word and get the answer! Don't mix up doubt with a false teacher's evil intentions. Doubt can be overcome. But once you have knowledge of the truth yet go on to dishonor Christ by preaching another Jesus and a different gospel, you've become a false teacher.

Peter said that false teachers "deny the Lord who bought them" (2 Peter 2:1). First, let me explain what this does not mean. You may have had opportunities to speak up about Jesus but declined to do so because of the pressure of what others might think. And you are beating yourself up, wondering, *Did I commit blasphemy of the Holy Spirit or commit the unforgivable sin?* You did not. Consider that experience as a learning lesson and fortify yourself with God's Word because it will produce confident faith, and faith makes for a bolder witness.

Failing to tell others about Jesus is not the denial false teachers engage in. False teachers are committed to giving their audience what they want to hear by any means possible—even if it means contradicting the Bible. First, they do a little analytical work on what's trending. They'll hone in on topics surrounding felt needs to craft messages that claim that by becoming a Christian you will be healthy, wealthy, and successful. All you need is a little faith.

The goal is to get under your skin, into your head, and touch your heart with *some* biblical truth. But you will never hear the full counsel of God, book by book, verse by verse, because that would disrupt their plans.

Every word of the Bible is essential, especially when it forewarns of deception, even within the church. Paul's warning to Timothy is one of those alerts. "The Spirit expressly says that in latter times some will depart from the faith, giving heed to deceiving spirits and doctrines of demons, speaking lies in hypocrisy, having their own conscience seared with a hot iron" (1 Timothy 4:1-2).

Believers need to open their eyes to the fact that there are pastors giving in to deceiving spirits—invisible entities with demonic doctrines—and taking their congregations with them. If that sounds sinister, it's because it is. Their conscience—their sense of right and wrong, truth and error—is numb to the Holy Spirit reaching out to them with truth because they were never born again (1 John 2:19).

Watch Out for Killers of the Soul

A pastor can be charismatic and wildly popular and be the definition of a false teacher and prophet. One such pastor was asked during an interview some simple questions regarding faith. His answers highlighted how deceivers twist and manipulate the truth.

When asked about the character of God in relation to a tragic earthquake, he sidestepped the question but made a telling statement regarding what he called the "dominant story" (his words, not mine) of the Scriptures. It's about a God who insists amidst chaos that the last word hasn't been spoken yet. Wait! What was he implying? With that one comment, he sowed seeds into unsuspecting minds that any inspiration coming to him is because God's last word hasn't been spoken yet. He directly contradicted Hebrews 1:1: "God, who at various times and in various ways spoke in time past to the fathers by the prophets, has in these last days spoken to us by His Son." God is done speaking, and to say anything else is willfully deceitful.

The reporter also questioned the pastor about a theological firestorm he had ignited. He believes that our response to the gospel in this life doesn't necessarily determine our eternal destiny. And that based on God's love, all people will be saved, even those who have rejected the claims of Christ. This is universalism, yet that pastor denies being a universalist. He claims that others need to see that the Christian message has *many different options*. What he should have said is that there is only one way to be saved (John 14:6; Acts 4:12).

The moment you imply that there are different paths, you deny Christ, refute Scripture, and gut the gospel.

Like a dog refusing to give up a bone, the reporter repeated the question: "Is it immaterial or irrelevant how one responds to Christ in this life in terms of determining one's eternal destiny? Does it have a bearing?" The pastor's answer: "It has tremendous bearing, but it also raises all sorts of questions. Namely, what about people who haven't heard about Jesus?"[4] I wanted to shout, "Stop right there! What about Romans chapter 1?"

Romans 1:20 assures us that every person has enough awareness of the eternal Godhead so that those who reject God are without excuse. Even tribespeople living in the deepest, darkest Amazon jungle can sense the Creator's handiwork around them in the colors, sights, and sounds of the animals, scenery, and sky above. Creation speaks of God when a missionary cannot.

As far as I know, the interviewer was not a believer, but he hit the nail squarely on the head when he said, "You've amended the gospel so that it is palatable to contemporary people who find the idea of heaven and hell difficult to stomach."[5]

Fast-forward two years, and once again this influential pastor publicly cast doubt on the authority and relevance of Scripture by validating same-sex partnerships. He said that the apostle Paul didn't have a "cultural framework," and wasn't talking about what we're talking about today, which is two people in a committed same-sex relationship. Yet the Bible groups homosexuality, fornication, and adultery into the camp of unsanctioned sex (1 Corinthians 6:9). The cultural acceptance of sin should never be allowed to override the veracity of God's Word. Unfortunately, droves of young people follow this teacher. Countless souls are being led straight into perdition—hell—because they are following the destructive ways that he, and others like him, portray as acceptable.

Look past the cool clothes and big personality, past the cross or cleric's collar, and many times you'll discover a cold-blooded killer of the soul. Why? False teaching is fatal even if its morbidity has not yet been manifested.

The days we're living in require us to be discerning about where we put our foot and where we sit down, spiritually speaking. Pray and pick your church carefully. Large followings can give a sense of approval, which isn't always a good thing. Scripture uses the word "many" to describe followers of false teachers—people who imitate and replicate others just like them (see 2 Peter 2:2). It has been said that "crowds gather around crowd gatherers," which is fine if they sell blenders at a fair. But when someone with an evil intent gathers others and teaches false doctrines, he or she is trafficking in the world of the souls of men, and heaven and hell are invisibly waging war in that reality.

Many may come into a false teacher's congregation, but God's people will not often stay long-term because the teacher's inspirational messages have no power when life gets tough. One week, a congregant can walk through the church doors on top of the world, and the next, in despair over unexpected news. A son was arrested, a spouse cheated, a layoff notice came, or the doctor said it doesn't look good—none of that makes sense in the world false teachers promote. Health, wealth, and prosperity messages cannot offer anything more than rosy platitudes, while the entirety of Scripture guarantees that we can face any adversity with calm assurance. Because Jesus triumphed over sin and the pain and suffering it causes, He can and will help us in our time of need.

Paul's command to "preach the word! Be ready in season and out of season. Convince, rebuke, exhort, with all longsuffering and teaching" (2 Timothy 4:2) isn't limited solely to pastors and teachers. Those words apply to all Christians, but especially to God's pulpits. Pastors and teachers are supposed to give the good news and the tough news—that which is comforting as well as disconcerting because the truth builds bold faith!

Watch Out for Exploiters

Decades ago, while on a family vacation, my parents stopped in the middle of the California desert to get gas and so we could stretch our legs. We kids were goofing off near train tracks and could see the light of a train in the distance. Soon, we could feel the vibrations on the rails. We stayed close enough to the tracks to see the full extent of what was coming our way—a little too close. The thought occurred to us, *We'd better jump back, and quick*. We watched as the train sped by, sucking up dust, twigs, and debris underneath its cars. I could feel that same suction pulling me toward the wheels, and let me tell you, it scared me to death.

I learned a valuable lesson that day that can apply to false teachers. It isn't a stretch to say they are like a speeding train and will suck you in if you let them. They do it because of covetousness (2 Peter 2:3). Their desire for fame and fortune is insatiable, and you are like merchandise to them, a market to conquer. They will prostitute you spiritually to get what they want physically. Be careful, be wise, or you will become an easy mark. And hold on to your wallet because if you don't understand God's view of money, they will take it too.

Paul wrote to the Corinthian believers, "He who sows sparingly will also reap sparingly, and he who sows bountifully will also reap bountifully" (2 Corinthians 9:6). And Proverbs 11:25 says, "The generous soul will be made rich, and he who waters will also be watered himself." Both verses show that giving—i.e., sowing and reaping—is a spiritual law, yet the amount you give is between you and God. "Let each one give as he purposes in his heart, not grudgingly or of necessity; for God loves a cheerful giver" (2 Corinthians 9:7).

Exactly how cheerful is a cheerful giver? According to the original New Testament language, we're to give with a hilarious heart. It should be sheer joy to offer to God a portion of what He has blessed us with. Does that mean we'll get a lot back if we give a lot of money? Not necessarily. The blessings could be health, peace, or joy. No earthly man can define what God's dividends pay. So why give to God at all? We give because He commands it (Proverbs 3:9). God doesn't need our money, but giving helps us keep a proper perspective of our resources. God invites us to invest in His kingdom, yet He provides for ministries as He sees fit, often in ways that defy explanation.

Ministries bound up in covetousness brazenly exploit people by means of deceptive words. The Greek word for "deceptive" is *plastos*, from which we get our word *plastic*. I am old enough to remember when Hot Wheels and Matchbox cars were mostly metal rather than plastic. The original die-cast cars were durable and fast. Nowadays, they're light as a feather. They are mostly molded plastic—a far cry from the original—much like deceptive words. In the rush to gain followers, false teachers use God's Word to tickle listeners' itching ears (2 Timothy 4:3), just like the false prophets in Jeremiah's day.

In Jeremiah 14:14, the Lord declared, "The prophets prophesy lies in My name. I have not sent them, commanded them, nor spoken to them; they prophesy to you a false vision, divination, a worthless thing, and the deceit of their heart." The false prophets were telling people everything was going to be fine. "Don't worry about God's judgment," they said. Their message wasn't so dissimilar to the "Tell me what I want to hear" attitude of the so-called Christian community today. And God says, "I'm not in it."

Poor Jeremiah was only a teenager when God called him to give a tough message. Jeremiah determined to keep his mouth shut—until God's words burned like fire, and he couldn't hold them back (Jeremiah 20:9). Jeremiah knew his message wouldn't be received well, and it wasn't. Neither will ours when we courageously stand against false teachers, but we can't let that stop us.

Judgment Is Coming!

Christianity is all about caring for and loving others, while false teachers think only of self, to their condemnation. Jude 1:12 calls them "late autumn trees without fruit, twice dead." They have nothing to offer because they're twice dead. I love how the Jewish mind thinks. Dead is only mostly dead. But twice dead—now that is dead!

The Bible talks about being twice dead in Revelation 21:8: "The cowardly, unbelieving, abominable, murderers, sexually immoral, sorcerers, idolaters, and all liars shall have their part in the lake which burns with fire and brimstone, which is the second death." This judgment is reserved exclusively for those who have rejected Christ and is irreversible. But false teachers don't believe they're going to hell, either because they deny its existence, or they think it's metaphorical. Nonetheless, "their judgment has not been idle, and their destruction does not slumber" (2 Peter 2:3). That is one terrifying promise! Judgment is on its way like a package, sealed, stamped, and en route.

Why such harsh condemnation? Neglect of the cross. Altar calls that emphasize putting your faith in Jesus because God loves you but make no mention of repentance from sin blatantly omit the horrific, bloody cross. Preaching that neglects the cross as the means by which your sins are forgiven gives false hope and leads people astray.

Every single time Jesus and the disciples preached the gospel, they all said the same thing in the same chronological order. Repent and believe in the Lord Jesus Christ, and you will be saved. Repent is *metanoia* in the Greek text, and it means to have a different thought—a 180-degree change of thinking about who Christ is. When you think differently about Jesus, it opens the door to Him becoming your Lord and Savior. But you won't realize your need for a Savior until you recognize that you are a sinner. And therein is the problem—a lot of people aren't convinced that they're sinners.

Have you ever had a lustful thought or cheated on your spouse inwardly, even once? You're a sinner. Have you been quick-tempered or said unkind words? You're a sinner. How about thinking you were better than someone else or stealing a cookie as a kid when your mom wasn't looking? To these questions and more, the answer is sinner! No one goes to heaven unless they first recognize that they are a sinner in need of saving. To believe anything other than the gospel truth condemns you to the darkest eternity imaginable. The awful reality of hell is why we must come against teachers who refuse to tell the truth.

What if pastors and teachers stopped caring about popularity or social media criticisms and instead preached the gospel and taught the Scriptures? What would happen if Christians took a stand for righteousness's sake? It is not too late. As long as we have breath, history remains to be written.

> One Christian standing against evil is all God needs to do a great work. Never underestimate the power of your voice when you courageously stand for God's truth.

From the earliest written account found in the Ecclesiastical History by Theodoret, Bishop of Cyrrhus,[6] to President Ronald Reagan's retelling at the National Annual Prayer Breakfast in 1984,[7] the account of a lowly ascetic monk named Telemachus has captivated the hearts and minds for thousands of years, and for good reason. Historical accounts vary concerning minor details, but the core of his actions is indisputable.

In the early AD 400s, Telemachus, a Roman citizen, and Christian, went to the Colosseum to watch the gladiatorial games for the first time. As he watched one man attempting to slay another, Telemachus was so offended by the human carnage that he jumped from the crowd into the arena, ran to the two gladiators, and stopped them where they stood. He pleaded, "Do not requite God's mercy in turning away the swords of your enemies by murdering each other!"

Accounts vary as to whether it was the angry crowd or the gladiators, but Telemachus was slain on the spot.

This moment might appear a wasteful tragedy, but it isn't the end of the story. When told of the scene, the Roman emperor Honorius was profoundly moved and ended the gladiatorial games—banishing them from Rome forever.

One man. One Christian standing against evil is all God needs to do a great work. Never underestimate the power of your voice when you courageously stand for God's truth.

CHAPTER 7

IN YOUR SIGHTS

Deceivers don't start out in the pulpit—they first sit in the pew. Some never stand in front of a congregation, but they are no less dangerous, which means we need to examine every bit of biblical instruction about them. Anyone or anything that leads people away from biblical doctrine leads them away from eternal life. That is a serious issue because the act of dying, that last breath, is but a moment, while hell is a perpetual existence for the lost. What a sobering thought, especially when it concerns loved ones who have rejected Jesus. I know this because my sister, Peggy, was once one of them.

Peggy was one of the most precious people you would ever want to meet. She loved everybody. Her heart and mind were wide open—too open. My sister was into crystals and Ouija boards. She was pantheistic and worshipped many gods. In Peggy's mind, when the end came, if she had dabbled in a bit of everything, she would be okay. A lot of people think like that—until reality hits.

I was teaching at a Bible college when Peggy called and asked, "Can you come by my house today?" After I arrived, she announced, "I have cancer, and they tell me it's pretty bad. Will you pray for me?" I thought, *This is wild*. I had told her about Jesus for years, but she had the luxury of refusing Him. But now, in this life-threatening crisis, none of her spirituality could bring her hope. I prayed and shared the gospel with her again, and this time it was different. The reality of death had hit her hard. Suddenly, everything she'd had the liberty of entertaining amounted to nothing. She needed Christ, His forgiveness, and His power over death.

Peggy immediately responded to the gospel, repented of her sins, and accepted Jesus as her Lord and Savior. She went on to live seven more years, but they were not pleasant. Yet amidst all the chemotherapy, surgeries, and Gamma Knife procedures, I watched my sister be transformed as she gravitated more and more toward the Word of God. On the day of her death, Peggy could not wait to see Jesus—her Redeemer lived, and she knew it.

Jesus said, "Enter by the narrow gate; for wide is the gate and broad is the way that leads to destruction, and there are many who go in by it. Because narrow is the gate and difficult is the way which leads to life, and there are few who find it. Beware of false prophets" (Matthew 7:13-15). Notice that false prophets are directly connected to the broad way to hell, which is why we need to set them in our sights and determine to catch, defeat, and overcome them.

WE CANNOT IGNORE THE FACTS

Founding Father John Adams famously said, "Facts are stubborn things; and whatever may be our wishes, our inclinations, or dictates of our passions, they cannot alter the state of facts and evidence."[1] That is never truer than when you examine the facts surrounding false teachers. With so many challenges facing the church today—declining attendance, social issues, and gender confusion among them—why focus on false teachers? Can't we simply ignore them? No, we cannot. Increasingly, there are pastors and teachers who say one thing publicly, but deep down inside, something is very wrong. Wait long enough and their conduct will expose them in due time (Numbers 32:23), but not before they destroy people.

False prophets and teachers have become adept at presenting themselves in venues outside of the church, and many believers are being duped as they allow these imposters to infiltrate their lives. At the risk of being perceived as a broken record and a dinosaur rolled into one, my exhortation is this: Use discernment when you read and watch stuff on the internet. Much of social media is not your friend when it comes to spiritual issues. Make sure the people you are following are legitimate believers when held up to the judgment of God's Word.

In the last days, the Bible says there will be deceivers everywhere. They will entice Christians to believe in falsehoods. This is one of the reasons unbelievers criticize the church today. They see what deceivers are doing, and they say those who listen to them are like a bunch of lemmings, blindly falling into line like little automatons. Unbelievers make statements like that because, in their eyes, that is what we are. Yet, how often has it been revealed that these same people were duped by a self-described expert's faulty, or worse, fraudulent research?

The fact remains that, knowingly or unknowingly, someone or something influences each of us. And if we are to avoid being labeled as mindless conformists, we must be wise concerning those who should be exposed and avoided.

HOW BAD COULD THEY BE?

They Are Prideful

How do we begin to identify and unmask the dangerous teachers and false prophets around us? It helps to know that their number one characteristic is pride—that's one way we can recognize them.

Now, we all struggle with pride. It's inherent to our fallen nature. I know you might disagree because you don't see yourself as boastful or arrogant, but as we saw in the case of Satan, it is the foundation of *all* sin. Pride is deeply rooted within us and is perhaps the most dangerous sin of all. And yet it is so cleverly disguised that we often don't recognize it for what it is. I believe there are times when we even applaud a form of pride in Christian ministries by letting everything center on some form of Christian celebrity. Pride is the antithesis of humility, a characteristic that God and the Holy Spirit desire for those in ministry.

We naturally gravitate toward strong leaders, but when leadership is authoritative, demanding, and attention-grabbing, it becomes something altogether different. In my mind, I can see a kaleidoscope of faces from my television screen—proud, authoritative, condescending ministers who ask, push, and promote themselves. This is not godly leadership.

A false teacher's proud spirit cannot be hidden. Inevitably, their pride will be manifest in their conduct. Second Peter 2:10 says such teachers will "walk according to the flesh in the lust of uncleanness and despise authority. They are presumptuous, self-willed." Peter uses the word "uncleanness" to describe false teachers, and as bad as that sounds, the original Greek language is far more graphic. They have a rotten stench of decay about them, similar to what you would expect from a putrid, stagnant pit, but they are oblivious to their condition. "Pride blinds the mind, distorts the vision, and so inflates the ego that the person can't tell the truth from fiction."[2]

The false teacher's disdain for authority is not surprising. Some Bibles rightly translate the word "authority" in verse 10 as "governments," but in this context, it could also mean they despise spiritual authorities. In other words, they have no respect for the things of God, and it shows. According to Romans 13:1, every soul is to be "subject to the governing authorities. For there is no authority except from God, and the authorities that exist are appointed by God." Secular governments and their agents, such as law enforcement officers and firefighters, are God-ordained authorities. Yet false teachers have a self-appointed authority that is contemptuous of all authority, secular or spiritual, that God has put in place, which is indicative of pride.

They Are Presumptuous

Adding to the list of characteristics in 2 Peter 2:10, false teachers are "presumptuous," which means to be reckless with your body or self-abusing. It also means to take your existence—who you are—and throw yourself at life with reckless abandon and little regard for the value of your life or the lives of others. Their presumptuous attitude endangers themselves and others. They cannot hold themselves back from giving in to their passions. Once they leave the studio or pulpit, they indulge their appetite for spending, sexual escapades, drunkenness, or even drug abuse, all the while using Scripture to justify their actions.

When warned against following those types, people often say, "I hear you, but no matter what my pastor does, it will never sway me to do anything ungodly." But King Solomon asked, "Can a man take fire to his bosom, and his clothes not be burned?" (Proverbs 6:27). Of course not! Believer, be wise regarding your acceptance of a spiritual leader's sin.

When you give sin an inch, it will take a mile. And if you allow an appetite to prevail, inevitably, it takes over, making it imperative that we control our private parts—or, as Romans 6:13 calls them, members. "Do not present your members as instruments of unrighteousness to sin, but present yourselves to God as being alive from the dead, and your members as instruments of righteousness to God."

The moment you read the words *private parts*, an image likely entered your mind, but that thought, or picture, probably missed the mark. Your most private parts are inward and have to do with your mind, eyes, and ears. You can be humming praise music all day long, but if you enter a grocery store and you hear a Top 10 song, guess which song is more likely to stick in your mind? That's right:

the secular one with the catchy tune. Why is that? Our minds are like sponges, which is why we are commanded to gird or tighten them up by exercising self-control (1 Peter 1:13).

What you allow your mind and body to indulge in is serious business because "you were bought at a price; therefore glorify God in your body and in your spirit, which are God's" (1 Corinthians 6:20). We understand from the verses immediately preceding that Paul was referring to sexual activity, but the scope of his words is not limited to that. It can be anything that causes you to depart from God. He gifted you your body, and if you are using it for any sort of unrighteousness, stop.

Christian, every part of our being belongs to God, yet there are people claiming to be God's representatives who are living aberrant lifestyles. Regarding these types, J. Vernon McGee's assessment is golden: "This is a picture of those who are lower than animals."[3] Having been created in the image of God, they have taken themselves out of the domain of human and have become vicious, vile, and violent. Wherever they go, left in their wake is destruction. Romans 3:10-18 puts it like this:

> There is none righteous, no, not one;
> there is none who understands;
> there is none who seeks after God.
> They have all turned aside;
> they have together become unprofitable;
> there is none who does good, no, not one.
> Their throat is an open tomb;
> with their tongues they have practiced deceit;
> the poison of asps is under their lips;
> whose mouth is full of cursing and bitterness.
> Their feet are swift to shed blood;
> destruction and misery are in their ways;

and the way of peace they have not known.
There is no fear of God before their eyes.

This passage applies to all humanity and defines the age we are living in, but it is especially true of false teachers whose reigning authority in life is self. They have no fear of God and have departed from Him.

When someone departs from God, how good or bad can that man or woman be? Answer: very bad! Humanity is good when people act like God—compassionate, caring, and kind. Yet when they depart from Him and His ways, they can outdo a demon.

They Are Depraved

The Bible paints a very graphic picture of the false teacher's current state, condemnation, and future destruction:

> They are not afraid to speak evil of dignitaries, whereas angels, who are greater in power and might, do not bring a reviling accusation against them before the Lord. But these, like natural brute beasts made to be caught and destroyed, speak evil of the things they do not understand, and will utterly perish in their own corruption (2 Peter 2:10-12).

Man will curse God and other men, and men will curse those in the spiritual realm, but here, the point being made is that not even angels will do those kinds of things. Jude 1:9 says Michael, the archangel, and Satan were arguing over the dead body of Moses. Even though Michael was contending with Satan, he didn't say, "I rebuke you." Instead, he said, "The Lord rebuke you!" Have you ever seen someone on television hold their hand up and rebuke the devil, and encourage you to do the same? Those teachers have no authority to do that, and what they are spewing will come back upon them and be part of their demise.

This next statement is strong and terrible. But the Bible says it, which means we need to hear it. False teachers are like "brute beasts made to be caught and destroyed." There are violent, animal-like, and godless people walking the earth and making mischief. Your temptation is probably the same as mine, and that is to ask, "Why doesn't someone do something?" I agree someone should do something, and that someone is us.

We must forcefully but civilly say to not only false teachers but also the brute who beats his wife and makes excuses, "God is in hot pursuit of you." To the child abuser, we must say, "God is in hot pursuit of you." We must remember that God is holy and righteous. He is a just judge and angry with the wicked every day (Psalm 7:11). When you are perpetrating evil and you think you are getting away with it, remember, God is in hot pursuit of you. A friend of mine likes to use the phrase "like white on rice." To be on someone like white on rice is to watch that person closely. That is how God acts when evil is afoot.

The idea that God goes after evildoers is as frightening as it is true. Every one of us has a God-given responsibility for our actions. You can completely deny the existence of God and still possess a standard of morality. We are spiritual beings created in God's image with a moral consciousness. In other words, regardless of whether you are a follower of God or a full-blown atheist, you have a concept of right and wrong. Yet very few people stop and ask the question, "Where does that innate understanding come from?" Romans 2:15 tells us that God's law is written upon every person's heart, and their conscience bears witness to it.

Humans have a moral rudder and know the difference between right and wrong. Why do I bring this to your attention? Because false teachers have forsaken the right way—God's way—to go astray. They know the truth, can recite the truth, and may have taught the truth at one time, but at some point, they loosened their grip on it. They let the truth slip right out of their hand, initiating a spiritual decline and a series of surrenders. To those people, Hebrews 6:4-6 says, "It is impossible for those who were once enlightened, and have tasted the heavenly gift, and have become partakers of the Holy Spirit, and have tasted the good word of God and the powers of the age to come, if they fall away, to renew them again to repentance, since they crucify again for themselves the Son of God, and put Him to an open shame."

The key here is that these teachers tasted God's goodness—they saw Him work, felt the emotion of the moment, and thought, *Wow, this is fantastic*, only to turn away. Because of the extent of their rejection of the Son of God, it is impossible to bring such people back to repentance. By their rejection, they have nailed Him to the cross once again, holding Him up to public shame.

There are some who use this Hebrews passage to say you, as a Christian, can lose your salvation. But the ones in jeopardy of being forsaken castaways are those who heard the gospel and experienced God moving, but it was never rooted and grounded in them. They professed to be participants in spiritual activity yet were nothing more than spectators. They acquiesced to the gospel by saying things like, "That's good. I approve. It's a good way to live. Excellent principles, and yes, Jesus died on the cross for my sins." They agreed but never lived it.

Hebrews 4:1-2 says, "Since a promise remains of entering His rest, let us fear lest any of you seem to have come short of it. For indeed the gospel was preached to us as well as to them; but the word which they heard did not profit them, not being mixed with faith in those who heard it." How does that happen? Two people hear the same sermon, on the same day and at the same time, but one misses out because what they heard was not mixed with faith. And by faith, I mean saving faith that rests fully upon Jesus Christ alone. They came near to Jesus for a season—we don't know how long that season was—but eventually they went back to their old system of works. Their belief never took them to saving faith; thus, they were never born again.

Hebrews 4:1-2 and 6:4-6 imply that if you shut the door on the gospel, your actions say, "This doesn't work. I've already tried Jesus, and He doesn't work. I guess I'm going to form my own belief system." And that is the foundation that leads to every man doing what is right in his own eyes. This is not about people who had salvation and lost it. It is about those who expressed belief but never moved to faith. Preachers, ministers, and evangelists are not exempt from that reality.

Even though we are examining the characteristics of false teachers, this is a good time to do a self-check. Scripture declares, "The time has come for judgment to begin at the house of God" (1 Peter 4:17), and that means it begins with us first. The focus of this judgment is not the believer's sins—God laid those upon Christ at the cross. We must allow the Word of God to examine and judge our actions and motives (Hebrews 4:12). Like any good cleansing agent, Scripture will sting, and maybe even hurt, but in these dark days, we need to be extremely careful concerning our walk with Jesus. Ask yourself: "Do any of these statements reflect my relationship with Jesus Christ?"

- I accepted Christ, said I believed, but have yet to live out my profession of faith.
- I was closer to Jesus last year than I am now.
- I am on the backside of the curve, spiritually speaking.
- I have given up on one or more of the following: prayer, Bible reading, witnessing.
- I am not serving God by serving my brothers and sisters in Christ. Nor am I giving from my resources monetarily.

If you answered yes to any of the above statements, return! "Remember therefore from where you have fallen; repent and do the first works" (Revelation 2:5). Hold on to Jesus, and don't loosen your grip!

They Go from Bad to Worse

In 2 Peter 2, the characteristics of false teachers go from bad to worse. Filled with pride, forsaking the righteous way, and having gone astray, they also follow "the way of Balaam the son of Beor, who loved the wages of unrighteousness" (verse 15). The way of Balaam is one of compromise. Technically, Balaam didn't execute a crime, which might lead you to ask, "If he didn't do anything overtly bad, why is he condemned as a bad guy?" Good question. Let me ask one in return: How many people are in ministry today that others say of them, "I don't see how they could be considered a false prophet or teacher"? The answer lies in the motives of the heart.

Balaam's account may be thousands of years old, but it holds real-life application for every believer, in every age. I encourage you to read the whole record of Balaam in Numbers 22–24, but for now, let's take a brief look at how this prophet relates to the modern-day church.

Balak, the pagan king of the Moabites, was looking for someone to curse the Moabites' Jewish enemies and was willing to pay to get the job done, so he turned to Balaam. Balak sent his request through messengers, and Balaam responded to it, which was his first mistake. As a prophet, Balaam was supposed to speak for God, so Balaam replied, "I can't do what you are asking. I can only say what God puts in my mouth." That cover story made him look good, but there was something ugly hiding inside.

Although Balaam declined Balak's request, he kept dialoguing with him—another mistake—and eventually he relented, saddled up his donkey, and went off to see the king. And then the unexpected happened.

Balaam's donkey was walking along minding her own business and carrying the false prophet on her back—until she saw the Angel of the Lord standing in her path (Numbers 22:23). Can you imagine? I wonder what animals see that we can't. In this case, the donkey sees the Angel, and wanting to avoid Him, she goes off the road into a field, prompting Balaam to beat her. Next, the donkey pushes up against a wall, crushing the prophet's foot. He beats her again. Finally, the donkey resorts to lying down under Balaam, and yes, he responds by beating her with his staff. What happened next, only the Lord could do. He opened her mouth to speak.

According to the Bible, Balaam was "rebuked for his iniquity: a dumb donkey speaking with a man's voice restrained the madness of the prophet" (2 Peter 2:16; see also Numbers 22:22-32). I have no idea what a donkey's voice might sound like, but this reminds me of the 1960s sitcom featuring Mister Ed, the talking horse, and Wilbur, his owner. The show was a silly comedy, but this situation was anything but funny. It was deadly serious. The donkey asked Balaam, "What have I done to you, that you have struck me these three times?...Am I not your donkey on which you have ridden, ever since I became yours, to this day? Was I ever disposed to do this to you?" (Numbers 22:28, 30). Balaam answered no, and the Lord opened his eyes to see the Angel of the Lord standing in the way with His sword drawn and ready to kill him (verse 31). The donkey wasn't so dumb after all. She saved Balaam's life!

The Angel of the Lord withstood the prophet because his way was "perverse" before Him (verse 32). Why? Because Balaam's motive for helping a pagan king was money. He loved money and what it offered. If Balaam were alive today, he would most likely be traveling with an entourage on black donkeys with tinted windows! Nothing but the best for a prophet!

Balaam was a greedy man, a compromiser who loved the wages of unrighteousness. And he had no problem leading others down that same wicked path. Sadly, this is an accurate depiction of many who fill church pulpits today. Theologian J.B. Phillips translates the Bible's description of these men like this:

These are the men who delight in daylight self-indulgence; they are foul spots and blots, playing their tricks at your very dinner-table. Their eyes cannot look at a woman without lust, they captivate the unstable ones, and their techniques of getting what they want is, through long practice, highly developed. They are born under a curse, for they have abandoned the right road and wandered off to follow the old trail of Balaam, son of Peor, the man who had no objection to wickedness as long as he was paid for it (2 Peter 2:13-15).

In Jesus' letter to the church in Pergamos, we see how far a false prophet is willing to go to gain what they want. Jesus said they "hold the doctrine of Balaam, who taught Balak to put a stumbling block before the children of Israel, to eat things sacrificed to idols, and to commit sexual immorality" (Revelation 2:14). Balaam couldn't curse Israel, so he devised another plan that allowed him to circumvent God's will and get his money. He showed Balak how he could weaken the people of Israel, and make them an abomination to God, through the Moabite women camped nearby. The Jewish men were enticed by them and impregnated them, causing the holy line of the Jewish people to be contaminated. Israel did what God expressly forbade, and Balaam was responsible.

If Balaam had been a devoted prophet of God, he would have been content with God's presence and provision. Instead, he used religion and ministry as a means for personal gain. First Timothy 6:6 tells us that "godliness with contentment is great gain." That same passage goes on to warn, "The love of money is a root of all kinds of evil, for which some have strayed from the faith in their greediness, and pierced themselves through with many sorrows" (verse 10).

The love of money can be summed up in one word: greed. Money itself is not evil. Money can be incredibly holy when used the right way. It all depends on how you use it and what it is dedicated to. But the sin of Balaam, and those like him, is not about economics. Rather, it's about the thoughts, motives, and intents of the heart.

FORTIFY YOURSELF

Balaam was condemned because he forsook the right way by turning his back on God—to the point where there was no going back. Likewise, false teachers and prophets are a judged group of people because of their demonic doctrines and practices that produce spiritually anemic Christians. If you and I are recreational Christians, the frail, flimsy faith we've cultivated will become our experiential reality. We must separate ourselves from these types!

> God means for you to have a steadfast faith that never turns back.

Maybe the way of Balaam describes you today. You are toying with God as a cat plays with a mouse, and in your twisted perception, you are the cat. Or the Bible no longer excites you. It isn't enough, and you're searching for a word from another source. Sure, you handle Scripture from time to time, a little bit here and there, but the ways of the world still play a part of your life. Or perhaps you are causing others to sin for your benefit and pleasure. If anything of Balaam's way describes you, take heed! It is why your soul is tossed and turbulent, never at ease, and moving further and further from God.

If your spirit is troubled because you've recognized something of Balaam's way in yourself, and you are thinking, *I don't want to end up like these people—I want to be a true believer*, good! God means for you to have a steadfast faith that never turns back. But only you can make that change and thus make a difference.

I've said this to our church's congregation and now say it to you: Write the word *fortify* on a Post-it or notecard and put it somewhere prominent. Circle the word, highlight it, or do whatever it takes to remind yourself to bolster your spiritual borders and walls against the enticements of false teachers and their doctrines. Just in case you are unsure of what fortifying your life looks like, I have listed here five simple ways to strengthen yourself daily:

- Make the Bible your power source for life. Never look to a person, religion, or system to be your strength or access into the presence of God (2 Peter 1:2-3).

- Keep yourself in the love of God by walking closely with Jesus, who is God's love incarnate (Jude 1:21).

- Think about things that are true, noble, just, pure, lovely, of good report, virtuous, and praiseworthy—meditate on these things (Philippians 4:8). You'll feel as if spiritual water is flowing over you.

- "Seek those things which are above, where Christ is, sitting at the right hand of God. Set your mind on things above, not on things on the earth" (Colossians 3:1-2). Focus on what is eternal, which cannot be lost or taken away.

- Remember: You have been crucified with Christ; it is no longer you who live, but Christ lives in you; and the life that you now live in the flesh you are to live by faith in the Son of God, who loved you and gave Himself for you (Galatians 2:20).

Memorize the scriptures accompanying this list and embed them into your heart, mind, and soul with the intent to obey them. If you will do this, I promise that you will be unstoppable for the kingdom of God and against the darkness of this age. You will not be led astray.

Believer, do what is right, not what is convenient or to your benefit. Hang in there and keep on fighting the good fight of faith (1 Timothy 6:12). Others are counting on you.

CHAPTER 8

IT'S DARK OUT THERE

The sign posted by the Hawaiian Department of Transportation said "Warning! Possible Dangerous Conditions Ahead." As I drove past, I wondered what I was being alerted to. If I had been offered some context like Gusty Winds or Falling Rocks or Oncoming Traffic, Single Lane Ahead, then the caution sign would have had a more meaningful application. Warnings such as this make context and situational awareness critical. But what I was about to encounter could not have been what the sign meant. It happened on the road from Kapalua to the airport in Kahului on the island of Maui. Once I drove past the warning sign, the going got rougher as the roadway narrowed to a rutted one-lane passage hugging the mountainside along a steep cliff falling into the Pacific.

I drove cautiously, yet confident that I now had the sign's missing context—until I rounded a turn and encountered a large rock covered with native Hawaiian graffiti. Next to it was a pre-colonization tribal flag, various Polynesian icons, and wooden stakes with statements. But here is what gave emotion to the warning—a huge sacrificial boar had been gutted and placed on top of the rock. Later, I asked some of my island friends, "What was that all about?" They answered, "Pagan sacrifice." I expected scattered rocks on a slippery road, but this gave new meaning to the warning of dangerous conditions.

Today, you and I are navigating rocky, bumpy, and spiritually slippery roads where we'll encounter false doctrine, false teachers, demonic activity, and satanic worship. If we're going to survive these dangerous conditions, we need to have a greater understanding of what we're dealing with. I promise that by the end of this chapter, you will look at events taking place around you through a different lens.

THE DARK REALM

Scripture teaches that there are two distinct realms with guaranteed final outcomes. One is inhabited by the righteous—those who have come to experience the new life and illumination that Christ gives with the promise of heaven. The other is occupied by those whom Scripture calls the wicked, who are condemned to judgment and everlasting punishment. The Bible talks about the dark realm from cover to cover, yet by and large, the modern church, and sadly, pastors, gloss over it. For the most part, Christians have become accustomed to thinking primarily in physical terms—things you can touch and see. The challenge is getting believers to grasp the reality of the unseen world surrounding us.

According to Colossians 1:16, God created all things seen and unseen, visible and invisible. Every part of our world involves matter, from the smallest subatomic particles to the vast observable universe. The chair you may be sitting on is an arrangement of matter, as is my desk or your body. Physicists tell us that where there is matter, antimatter or dark matter also exists.

Scientists hold various theories on the nature of antimatter, but on this they agree: There is a world out there that is distinctly different from the physical universe you and I observe. Theoretically, there could be a train moving through the room where you are right now, and you would be oblivious to it because you are in a different molecular alignment. Robert Jastrow, an astronomer, planetary physicist, and former director of NASA's Goddard Space Center, wrote in *God and the Astronomers*,

> For the scientist who has lived by his faith in the power of reason, the story ends like a bad dream. He has scaled the mountains of ignorance; he is about to conquer the highest peak; as he pulls himself over the final rock, he is greeted by a band of theologians who have been sitting there for centuries.[1]

Jastrow was speaking in terms of creation, but we could also say that the scientific community caught up to what the Bible has said all along—we are surrounded by things that we cannot see.

Christians have a dark enemy who is hostile toward them, yet according to a Barna Group poll many will claim, "I believe in God, but I don't believe in a devil."[2] That statement is incompatible with biblical faith because the God they claim to believe in says there is a devil. Jesus knew that He was confronting the real devil and not a mere personification of evil in the Judean wilderness when Satan attempted to derail God's plan to redeem the souls of men (Luke 4:1-13).

Our true enemies are not human but, in fact, spirits. They are spiritual creatures from the dark realm that provide the inspiration and energy behind false teachers and prophets and their demonic doctrines. Their methodology is to operate without you realizing it, which makes their actions incredibly dangerous.

Satan's plot is to infiltrate the lives of humans, yet he can only hinder the spiritual growth of a believer. But if you are not a Christian, your life is open to demonic influence and even control. People have asked me if I really believe this. Yes, I do. Not only because I have seen undeniable, irrefutable evidence of demonic manifestations in people's lives, but more than my experience, Scripture says that Satan seeks a person's destruction in the same way a lion pursues its next meal. To some, that may sound disturbing, even shocking, and at some point, you may wonder, *Why do I need to know any of this information?* For this reason: Because the early church did.

The Bible records accounts of demonic activity in the Old Testament, and Jesus encountered demons and their work, as did New Testament believers who understood the realities of the unseen world. It is us who have regressed in our biblical knowledge and understanding.

Even with the abundance of books, programs, lectures, and seminaries in our day and age, biblical illiteracy is rampant despite scriptural warnings against being ignorant. Of great concern is the fact that many Christians are untaught regarding the Christian life (2 Corinthians 1:8), spiritual gifts (1 Corinthians 12:2), the rapture of the church (1 Thessalonians 4:13), and Israel's place in history and the future (Romans 11:25). It is especially disturbing that so many believers are ignorant of Satan's devices (2 Corinthians 2:11).

I appreciate how the apostle Paul lays out ignorance as a choice: "If anyone is ignorant, let him be ignorant" (1 Corinthians 14:38). Paul is talking about willful ignorance. I pray that isn't your mindset because if you are serving the Lord Jesus Christ, you are an enemy of hell's agenda. I believe that Satan wants nothing more than to see churches full of uninformed believers. He wants them ignorant of their enemy's presence, and by extension, his activities.

In Daniel 4:13, King Nebuchadnezzar tells Daniel the prophet, "I saw in the visions of my head while on my bed, and there was a watcher, a holy one, coming down from heaven." The word "watcher" refers to a spirit entity or spirit being. Some scholars read this verse as saying that the watcher was a good or holy watcher. Other scholars believe that there were two variants of watchers—one from the dark realm and the other from the heavenly realm, an angelic watcher. Regardless of the number or their origin, what is clear is that spiritual entities monitor human activity—some with good intent and others with evil. Jesus said, "I say to you, there is joy in the presence of the angels of God over one sinner who repents" (Luke 15:10). Angels witness people coming to Christ, and they rejoice, while the other side responds in fierce opposition to people becoming saved.

Daniel had firsthand knowledge of how demonic enemy forces operate. In Daniel chapter 10, he wrote about a spiritual war between demonic and angelic beings in the atmosphere, or heavenlies, over Persia, modern-day Iran. Daniel had been praying earnestly, and God dispatched an angel with the answer for Daniel, but the angel had difficulty breaking through the demonic forces to deliver the message:

> From *the first day* that you set your heart to understand, and to humble yourself before your God, your words were heard; and I have come because of your words. But the prince of the kingdom of Persia withstood me twenty-one days; and behold, Michael, one of the chief princes, came to help me, for I had been left alone there with the kings of Persia (Daniel 10:12-13).

The kings of Persia were demonic factions warring against God's heavenly hosts in the atmosphere. I hope this enlarges your understanding of what often takes place behind the scenes in the world around you.

THE FALLEN ANGELS

To truly understand the scope of the dark realm, we must go back to what God told the prophets Isaiah and Ezekiel concerning the original rebellion of Lucifer.

> Hell from beneath is excited about you,
> to meet you at your coming;

> it stirs up the dead for you,
> all the chief ones of the earth;
> it has raised up from their thrones
> all the kings of the nations…How you are fallen from heaven.
> O Lucifer, son of the morning!
> How you are cut down to the ground,
> you who weakened the nations! (Isaiah 14:9, 12).
>
> You were in Eden, the garden of God;
> every precious stone was your covering:
> the sardius, topaz, and diamond,
> beryl, onyx, and jasper,
> sapphire, turquoise, and emerald with gold.
> The workmanship of your timbrels and pipes
> was prepared for you on the day you were created.
> You were the anointed cherub who covers;
> I established you;
> you were on the holy mountain of God;
> you walked back and forth in the midst of fiery stones.
> You were perfect in your ways from the day
> you were created,
> till iniquity was found in you (Ezekiel 28:13-15).
>
> You have said in your heart:
> "I will ascend into heaven,
> I will exalt my throne above the stars of God;
> I will also sit on the mount of the congregation
> on the farthest sides of the north;
> I will ascend above the heights of the clouds,
> I will be like the Most High" (Isaiah 14:13-14).

When God created Lucifer and the angelic hosts, they were perfect. No one knows how many angels there are—it seems they are too numerous to count—or exactly when they were created. We assume they predate the creation of the physical universe because they were already present and sang praise to God at creation (Job 38:4, 7). What we do know for sure is that those same angels had the capacity to sin. Does that surprise you? It shouldn't. For worship and praise to be pure and true, it must originate from a free will, which means the angels possess the ability to choose and to sin.

According to Scripture, an envious, prideful, rebellious heart began to take root in Lucifer, leading him down a path from being God's anointed cherub to becoming Satan, the devil—the fallen angel cast from the presence of God. Lucifer's pride blinded him to the reality of God's holy judgment—this is the reason God made hell. But the devil won't go there alone. Though he was the instigator and prime offender in the heavenly revolt, Revelation 12:4, 9 tells us that other angels, having been deceived, followed his lead. "His tail [influence, power, cunning] drew a third of the stars of heaven and threw them to the earth...The great dragon was cast out, that serpent of old, called the Devil and Satan, who deceives the whole world; he was cast to the earth, and his angels were cast out with him."

Note: As we move forward regarding this topic, it is essential that we consult the Scriptures, which give us insight into what's ahead. In Job 1:6, we read that the sons of God (angels) appeared before the Lord in heaven. Again, in Job 2:1, the same is said regarding the sons of God as being angels. In Job 38:7, the angels are referred to as morning stars who sang God's praises at creation. In the Old Testament, the sons of God are always referred to as angelic creatures. Interestingly, humans are not called the sons of God in the Old Testament, only in the New Testament.

Satan and his fallen angels are free to create mischief and mayhem on earth, except for the angels mentioned in 2 Peter 2:4. "God did not spare the angels who sinned, but cast them down to hell and delivered them into chains of darkness, to be reserved for judgment." These angels receive a harsh condemnation.

Certain fallen angels committed sins so egregious that God had to intervene. He could not spare them. Used in this context, the word "spare" means God would not tolerate their behavior and had to act. The act that these angels committed was so wicked that God could not allow them to remain at large. He immediately had them seized and bound.

This binding or casting down was to a place called *Tartarus*, often referred to as *Hades* or the *abyss*. In verse 4, Peter uses *Tartarus*—a fascinating word that appears only here in the Bible. *Tartarus* is a place of shrouded imprisonment, a compartment in the depths of Hades. Worse than hell itself, it could be described as "the hellhole of Hell."[3] The severity of Peter's language here ought to open our eyes to the fact that we don't truly comprehend the deadly consequences of sin—how damning it is and the degree to which it offends the heart of God.

The book of Jude gives additional information to help us grasp the nature and magnitude of the fallen angels' sin, and why they are currently held in the darkest depths of hell:

> The angels who did not keep their proper domain, but left their own abode, He has reserved in everlasting chains under darkness for the judgment of the great day; as Sodom and Gomorrah, and the cities around them in a similar manner to these, having given themselves over to sexual immorality and gone after strange flesh, are set forth as an example, suffering the vengeance of eternal fire (Jude 1:6-7).

These angels "did not keep their proper domain." The word "domain" means atmosphere, home, dwelling, or arena. They left their own abode, dwelling place. What did these angels do? Both Jude and

Peter reference the correlation between Sodom and Gomorrah, sexual immorality, and strange flesh.

Scripture says that sexual relations between a male husband and a female wife are fantastic, holy, and a God-ordained blessing. The antithesis to God's design would be the union between unsanctioned physical flesh coming together. An unnatural, unsanctioned physical union of flesh—male to male, female to female, or human to animal—that brings judgment (see Romans 1:26-27; Exodus 22:19). It is my opinion that the unsanctioned sexual sin that God could not allow to continue was a sin of a particular kind. It was between fallen angels and female humans. This group of angels sinned so grossly against God and humanity that they are now held in chains and will not be released until the coming seven-year tribulation period.

How on earth did this happen? Here, it's best to let the Bible interpret the Bible because the answer will be hard to swallow for those unfamiliar with Genesis 6:1-4. Below, I have added biblical definitions where I felt they would help give a clearer sense of what took place:

> Now it came to pass, when men [descendants of Adam and Eve, mankind] began to multiply on the face of the earth, and daughters were born to them, that the sons of God [angel *bene-ha'elohim*] saw [*raah*: to stare, gaze, to follow] the daughters of men, that they were beautiful [*tob*: exciting, sensual, arousing]; and they took [*laqach*: carried away, caught, seized upon] wives [*ashiym, nawsheem*: a woman forced into sex, or being an adulteress] for themselves of all whom they chose [took, came upon, steal]. And the LORD said, "My Spirit shall not strive [put up with] with man forever, for he is indeed flesh; yet his days shall be one hundred and twenty years." There were giants [Nephilim] on the earth in those days, and also afterward, when [again] the sons of God [angel *bene-ha'elohim*] came

in to [seeded] the daughters of men and they bore children to them [angel *bene-ha'elohim*]. Those were the mighty men who were of old, men of renown.

Before we go any further, I want to segue for a moment. I believe there are holy angels, fallen angels, and demons. To make my point, let me make a few distinctions.

Angels, whether holy or fallen, are capable of appearing in human form. They never appear as or are connected to an animal or inanimate object. The New Living Translation of Hebrews 13:2 says, "Don't forget to show hospitality to strangers, for some who have done this have entertained angels without realizing it!" In other words, be nice to strangers. They might be angels. We also read throughout the Bible of angels speaking, taking people by the hand, eating, and engaging in physical combat (see Genesis 19:1).

It is my opinion that in contrast, demons appear to be distinctive from angels in that they are seemingly limited unless they have some form of habitation or host. It could be a human, animal, statue, or idol. Regardless, the unsuspecting host must be vacant, void, or empty of the indwelling of the Holy Spirit of God for this evil to take place. That is why it is impossible for Christians to be possessed (see 2 Corinthians 15:16). Do you think the Holy Spirit will move over and co-exist with a demonic spirit? Never! The devil and his ilk can certainly trouble believers, but we are to resist him, remain steadfast in the faith, and the enemy must flee from us (see James 4:7; 1 Peter 5:8-9).

According to the Bible, it also seems that demons seek dry places and avoid water. I know that sounds odd, and you may not have previously noticed this in the Bible, but here it is. "When an unclean spirit goes out of a man, he goes through dry places, seeking rest, and finds none" (Matthew 12:43). The English Standard Version says, "It passes through waterless places." Isn't it strange that in addition to looking for a body to inhabit, demons avoid water as if terrified of it? Have you ever wondered why the Holy Spirit took great pains to tell us these beings avoid water? I have, especially when reading about the cataclysmic flood God sent upon the earth.

These giants were unnatural genetic hybrids, the result of fallen angelic and human intercourse. That fact requires us to ask, Since they were not fully human nor entirely angelic, where did their spirits go upon their death in the flood?

Scripture does not give us the exact origin of demons, and several views have been put forth. Could it be that while God confined their spiritual existence to Tartarus because of their potentially ruinous effects on humanity, the disembodied spirits of these half-breeds became the origin of demons? I know some may disagree, but that is the only explanation that makes sense to me. Again, we must ask ourselves: If Genesis 6 is true, and it is, then what became of the half-breeds? We know God created angels, and whether they are holy or chose to rebel, they are still angels. But, nowhere in Scripture do we read of God creating demons.

In studying Genesis 6, 2 Peter, and Jude, I wrote myself this note: Why would such a Hollywood type of scenario with deviant angelic behavior happen? The answer goes back to Genesis 3:15: "I will put enmity between you and the woman, and between your seed and her Seed; He shall bruise your head, and you shall bruise His heel." From the beginning, God said that there would be enmity or warfare between Satan's progeny and the woman's progeny—Eve and her descendants.

Because God was speaking in both the eschatological sense (prophetic) and the soteriological (the doctrine of salvation), Genesis 3:15 should grab our attention. The original Hebrew word translated "seed" is *sperma*. Both seed and *sperma* carry information, but the difference is that "the Seed" of the woman gets a capital *S*, and Satan's does not. God promised that the coming Messiah would be of divine origin. The "sperm" that produced Jesus Christ in His incarnation had nothing of a human father present, exactly as the angel told Mary it would be. "The Holy Spirit will come upon you, and the power of the Highest will overshadow you; therefore, also, that Holy One who is to be born will be called the Son of God" (Luke 1:35).

Bible translators used the word "bruise" in Genesis 3:15, but a more accurate translation is *crush*. Which would you rather have crushed: your heel or your head? Satan was going to inflict tremendous pain on the Messiah at the cross and "bruise His heel," but the Messiah was going to crush Satan's head! Colossians 2:15 declares that Jesus Christ "disarmed principalities and powers, He made a public spectacle of them, triumphing over them."

Starting with Cain, Satan carried out demonic plans to stop the arrival of the Son God and the Father's plan of salvation, including the corruption of humanity. When one plan didn't work, he tried another, then another, and he is still at it today.

THE DAYS OF NOAH: THEN AND NOW

Most people like to skip over biblical genealogies, and I understand why, but I encourage you to resist the urge. Hidden among the long lists of difficult-to-pronounce names are nuggets of truth you won't want to miss. Such is the case with the genealogy of Noah, recorded by Moses in Genesis 6:9-10: "This is the genealogy of Noah. Noah was a just man, perfect in his generations. Noah walked with God. And Noah begot three sons: Shem, Ham, and Japheth." Noah's genealogy is short and sweet, but I want you to notice the word "perfect." It means physically sound, complete, intact, untainted, unblemished, and without fear. Noah was without physical defect. That is an unusual thing to say about him or anybody else, especially in a genealogy. And how does being physically sound relate to God's dealings with Noah?

The account of Noah and the ark is one of judgment *and* grace. Why, then, did God destroy the whole earth by flood? There are several reasons: men's thoughts were only evil continually, the earth was corrupt before God and filled with violence, and then there were the giants (Genesis 6:4). These giants are known in the Old Testament as the Rephaim, Nephilim, Arbathite, Zuzim, Karaim, Emim, and Anakim. The etymology of the Hebrew word *Nephilim* means the fallen ones. The English translation of the Hebrew *Emim* is the terrors, terrorizers, or tormentors, which is a description based on their powers, size, and looks. But remember, Noah was physically sound, and I believe genetically untainted.

Is it possible that Noah's lineage, his DNA, was not polluted by what was going on? How could this fall into the realm of possibility? Because in our era of DNA engineering and experimentation, we've learned that DNA can be altered.

Jesus told His disciples that there is a connection between what occurred in the past and what will take place in the future. He warned that the days prior to His second coming would mimic the days of Noah. "As the days of Noah were, so also will the coming of the Son of Man be" (Matthew 24:37). The level of demonically induced evil that Noah lived under would not exist again until the time of the end, when God will once again judge the earth. While it is true that this verse applies to the coming tribulation period, the unprecedented rise of two key indicators point to the fact that we are racing toward those days.

As in the days of Noah, deviant sexuality has become so prevalent that flags, festivals, parades, and an entire month are dedicated to proudly celebrating it. Even children are taught to accept, affirm, embrace, and transition. You need to ask yourself why. And why now?

In addition to that, US commercial and private pilots along with international aviation agencies regularly report strange atmospheric phenomena. The US government alone has reported hundreds of unidentified anomalous phenomena (UAP)—aberrations capable of appearing, disappearing, and maneuvering at extreme speeds outside our known laws of physics.[4] Are these from this world? I don't think so. The rise in these two abnormal activities leads me to believe they have demonic origins.

LIGHT WILL WIN

The realms of righteousness and wickedness are clashing. They are fighting in our families, marriages, and the halls of political power in our nation's Capitol—I've felt and seen it. Light and darkness are also warring in pulpits all around the world. We've witnessed the rise of false teachers who twist the gospel to fit their self-serving desires. Their corrupt teachings and hypocritical lifestyles are the evidence that Satan has infiltrated our churches. And because God previously condemned Satan and the fallen angels with their final judgment yet to come (Revelation 20:7-15), what can we conclude? God will surely judge anyone who robs you of the truth to blind you spiritually.

We must look beyond men's and women's faces and see the demonic powers behind them. Can you see the fur and fang, so to speak, flying left and right? Or are you acting as if nothing is happening in your town or home or church? If so, little do you know that spirit beings from another realm are instigating plans for your destruction or that of your marriage or family or congregation. You can't see that the refined people sitting in high places of authority over your children's education are being manipulated by powers bent on destroying their innocence. The sin, corruption, and demonic perversion they promote demand a response. We are at war! C.S. Lewis's insightful words give us an accurate assessment of this reality.

> Enemy-occupied territory—that is what this world is. Christianity is the story of how the rightful King has landed,

you might say landed in disguise, and is calling us all to take part in a great campaign of sabotage. When you go to church you are really listening-in to the secret wireless from our friends: that is why the enemy is so anxious to prevent us from going. He does it by playing on our conceit and laziness and intellectual snobbery. I know someone will ask me, "Do you really mean at this time of day, to re-introduce our old friend the devil—hoofs and horns and all?" Well, what the time of day has to do with it I do not know. And I am not particular about the hoofs and horns. But in other respects my answer is "Yes, I do." I do not claim to know anything about his personal appearance. If anybody really wants to know him better I would say to that person, "Don't worry. If you really want to, you will. Whether you'll like it when you do is another question."[5]

Where does this leave you? God has placed you squarely on the battlefield. Does all this seem fatalistic? It would, unless the Bible had shown you how to fight.

> Though we walk in the flesh, we do not war according to the flesh. For the weapons of our warfare are not carnal but mighty in God for pulling down strongholds, casting down arguments and every high thing that exalts itself against the knowledge of God, bringing every thought into captivity to the obedience of Christ, and being ready to punish all disobedience when your obedience is fulfilled (2 Corinthians 10:3-6).

Believer, it's evident that God calls us to boldness when we face Christ's enemies. Open your Bible and train your mind and heart to obey it. Go to your knees and pray like never before—God promises to answer. Be courageous and ready, and He will use you in a world that has turned its back on Him.

> All of God's promises to be your defense, shield, protector, lifter of your head, and to uphold you with His righteous right hand are yours to appropriate in every situation.

We've covered a fair amount of ground concerning the darkness weighing upon this world, and I want to lift the mood with some encouragement. While the unjust rightly tremble at the thought of God's future judgment (2 Peter 2:9), that should never be true about those of us who trust in Christ because we are eternally saved and sealed. "In Him you also trusted, after you heard the word of truth, the gospel of your salvation; in whom also, having believed, you were sealed with the Holy Spirit of promise, who is the guarantee of our inheritance until the redemption of the purchased possession, to the praise of His glory" (Ephesians 1:13-14). Being sealed by the Holy Spirit for the day of redemption is a seal that cannot be broken. There is no passage in the Bible that says you can be unsealed. What it does say is this:

> My sheep hear My voice, and I know them, and they follow Me. And I give them eternal life, and they shall never perish; neither shall anyone snatch them out of My hand. My Father, who has given them to Me, is greater than all; and no one is able to snatch them out of My Father's hand. I and My Father are one (John 10:27-30).
>
> Who shall separate us from the love of Christ? Shall tribulation, or distress, or persecution, or famine, or

nakedness, or peril, or sword? For I am persuaded that neither death nor life, nor angels nor principalities nor powers, nor things present nor things to come, nor height nor depth, nor any other created thing, shall be able to separate us from the love of God which is in Christ Jesus our Lord (Romans 8:35, 38-39).

That being true, all of God's promises to be your defense, shield, protector, lifter of your head, and to uphold you with His righteous right hand are yours to appropriate in every situation. God warned us these days would grind us down and wear us out (2 Timothy 3:1) so that we would be tired of standing for what is good and right and for what pleases God. But that doesn't mean we should quit! It means we stand up and keep moving forward. All of what we have been talking about proves that we are so very close to the finish line.

As a Christ-follower, you are safe in the hands of God the Father and God the Son. Think of yourself as safely tucked inside His powerful yet loving hands, never to be removed. Let that motivate you to go out and do what He has ordained for you!

CHAPTER 9

URGENT, URGENT, URGENT!

Our best intentions of obeying God's will often go awry because they are met by opposition, and we too soon give in to the spiritual powers luring us to do what we never intended. For instance, have you ever been nudged by God to act or speak in a certain way, but for some inexplicable reason, you didn't, or you did the opposite, and later you thought, *Why did I do that?* If you are like most people, you've done it more times than you'd care to admit. Even the eminent apostle Paul experienced these kinds of conflicts and expressed his frustration, saying, "What I will to do, that I do not practice; but what I hate, that I do" (Romans 7:15).

In the last chapter, we saw how the sway of the dark realm potentially influences believers and unbelievers alike. That awareness of the dark realm's reach should galvanize us with a sense of urgency to actively share God's concern about where people will spend eternity.

AN URGENT CALL

The Bible says, "The Lord is not slack concerning His promise, as some count slackness, but is longsuffering toward us, not willing that any should perish but that all should come to repentance" (2 Peter 3:9). God's unwillingness for any to perish doesn't mean He turns a blind eye to sinful conduct and allows people to go to heaven by default—quite the opposite! Humanity's default is hell. That truth hurts because it's meant to. God intervened by providing a way out of our predicament. He offered a way of escape, and He wants everyone to take it.

Jesus Christ went bloodied and bruised to the cross. He died, was buried, and rose victorious on the third day, wiping out "the handwriting of requirements that was against us, which was contrary to us. And He has taken it out of the way, having nailed it to the cross" (Colossians 2:14). Jesus destroyed the grip of hell. He canceled sin's power, erasing our guilt and shame!

Isaiah 6:1-8 is perhaps the most vivid portrayal of the effect of purged sins in the Old Testament. I've included it here because it describes what it means to come before a holy God, and it reveals the natural response to such an encounter.

> In the year that King Uzziah died, I saw the Lord sitting on a throne, high and lifted up, and the train of His robe filled the temple. Above it stood seraphim; each one had six wings: with two he covered his face, with two he covered his feet, and with two he flew. And one cried to another and said:
>
> > "Holy, holy, holy is the Lord of hosts;
> > the whole earth is full of His glory!"
>
> And the posts of the door were shaken by the voice of him who cried out, and the house was filled with smoke.
>
> So I said:
>
> > "Woe is me, for I am undone!
> > Because I am a man of unclean lips,

> and I dwell in the midst of a people of unclean lips;
> for my eyes have seen the King,
> the LORD of hosts."

Then one of the seraphim flew to me, having in his hand a live coal which he had taken with the tongs from the altar. And he touched my mouth with it, and said:

> "Behold, this has touched your lips;
> your iniquity is taken away,
> and your sin purged."

Also I heard the voice of the Lord, saying:

> "Whom shall I send,
> and who will go for Us?"

Then I said, "Here am I! Send me."

Isn't Isaiah's response amazing? Now forgiven, he says, "Here am I! Send me." Once you fully grasp the depth of God's forgiveness, you are willing to do whatever God asks. Isaiah's assignment was "Go and tell this people." Similarly, we've been commanded by God to go to our people and our culture in whatever city, state, and nation we live in. We are to speak and preach and talk and live and do all we can to show the world about our God. Our mission as Christians *is* urgent, and it requires a soldier's focus. Allow me to illustrate.

Put yourself on a helicopter lifting off from the flight deck of an aircraft carrier. You are on your way to execute a clandestine operation. The members of your team sit silently, side by side, mentally rehearsing every move from touchdown to wheels up—over and over. By now, continual practice has automated the actions and responses of every member. The team's cohesiveness goes beyond second nature; they are symbiotic—entirely in tune with one another.

Operators who support each soldier on that helo are watching over and caring for them by satellite, aircraft, on land, and at sea. They aren't in the direct line of fire, but they are just as focused on the mission at hand.

As those in the helo get closer to the target, all watches on board are synchronized to the second. Senses are heightened. Five minutes from touchdown, are any of those soldiers fantasizing about pornography, calculating their stock earnings, or regretting leaving their favorite video game behind? Do you think any of them would say, "You know what? I need one more drink or line of cocaine." Never! They absolutely do not think like that.

Now, are all these soldiers Christians? Of course not, and that is my point. In such a scenario, even a non-Christian soldier will not allow himself to be distracted in any way, shape, or form. Their focus is laser-sharp because the mission is everything and it screams of urgency. Success is the only option.

Far too many among us have lost the sense of urgency that comes with Jesus' commission to go and make disciples. We brush shoulders daily with those at the office, at school, around town, or on the subway, but if we could see hell stirring beneath our unbelieving coworkers and acquaintances, see it waiting with its mouth wide open, we would break down in tears. My intention isn't to condemn but to ask you to consider what is at stake. I am calling you to be focused on the mission God has given you. Will you, like Isaiah, say, "Here I am! Send me"?

The more you and I follow God, the more we will upset people, but we must be careful that our agenda is God's, not vice versa. President Abraham Lincoln wisely pointed this out during the Civil War. One of Lincoln's advisors said he was grateful God was on the Union's side. Lincoln replied, "Sir, my concern is not whether God is on our side; my greatest concern is to be on God's side, for God is always right."[1] I would also add that the world will not be on your side when you follow Christ with a depth of thought, commitment, and urgency. And I will go so far as to say that some would crucify you as they did Him, if they could.

If you believe that would never happen, perhaps it is time to adjust your thinking on what it means to think and act like Jesus. "I think Jesus is loving." He's loving all right, but this world doesn't understand one iota what true love is. Or maybe you imagine Jesus as a laid-back, nonconfrontational kind of guy. Where did that idea come from? It's not biblical. "Well, I believe He just wants me happy." Our English word *happy* comes from the archaic term *hap*, meaning "luck, chance, or good fortune." Using that definition, when things are going well, happiness results. It is true that God blesses us in countless ways that make us feel externally happy. But on a deeper, more internal level, He wants you holy regardless of external circumstances.

When I marry couples, I never say, "Fred, will you now say to Betty, 'I will make you happy the rest of your life?'" Instead, I turn to Fred and ask, "Fred, will you serve Betty all the days of your life? Are you willing to die for Betty from this moment forward by forsaking all others?" And then I turn to Betty and ask her the same. I do this because if your commitment in marriage, or anything else, is tied to circumstances, you will falter and most likely fail.

God isn't against happiness. Scripture says that He gives us "richly all things to enjoy" (1 Timothy 6:17). Happy is when you are eating an ice cream cone or getting a new puppy. But that feeling of happiness passes once you've eaten the last bite of the cone, or worse yet, the puppy snatches your ice cream from you. Jesus gives His children something far better than happiness. It's called joy.

The joy that Jesus had, He gives to us. "These things I have spoken to you, that My joy may remain in you, and that your joy may be full" (John 15:11). Circumstances may make you feel like your world has been blown apart, but in the midst, joy brings peace. You can be faced with seemingly insurmountable odds and still say, "But none of these things move me; nor do I count my life dear to myself, so that I may finish my race with joy, and the ministry which I received from the Lord Jesus, to testify to the gospel of the grace of God" (Acts 20:24).

Joy isn't the same as stoicism. It doesn't mean that we don't cry, aren't concerned, or don't experience sorrow. We are human. But joy allows us to remain unmoved and steadfast, which are essential if we want our lifestyle to send a message.

AN URGENT MESSAGE

Our mission is urgent because our lives pronounce judgment. Again, we see this clearly through the Old Testament example of Noah. Noah was blameless and correct in his motives and actions—in essence, he conducted himself righteously. But Noah wasn't perfect or sinless. Today, we might jokingly say Noah didn't walk on water, but then we would have to turn right around and confess that he loved God and walked with Him.

Every time I say, "I love Jesus," those words sound so shallow to me. They remind me of how little I really do love Him. When I say, "Lord, I love You," I immediately add, "O Lord, I pray that I would love You more." What I am really saying is, "I wish I obeyed You more." Noah's prevailing propensity was to do what God wanted because he loved God.

Jesus said that to love Him is to obey His commandments (John 14:21-23). When you're faced with a choice, do you obey God or your desires? Do people see your choices, big or small, as being radically different when compared to theirs? Are your choices driven by love for your Savior first, and then love for your fellow man?

Noah loved God, obeyed God, and walked with God. The definition of the Hebrew word translated "walk" is an encouragement to us all. It means to journey onward, keep moving forward, and not look back. Jesus said, "No one, having put his hand to the plow, and looking back, is fit for the kingdom of God" (Luke 9:62). We generally leave the task of plowing fields to professional farmers, but if you were plowing and you kept looking back, your furrows would end up crooked. The same principle applies to driving a car. As your head turns, it influences your upper body, turning the steering wheel, which affects your course. If you saw someone speeding down the freeway continually looking back, first over the right shoulder and then the left, their car will follow suit—swaying wildly from one side of the lane to the other.

Likewise, stop looking over your shoulder spiritually. Leave the past behind and keep going forward in Christ Jesus. I bring this up because once God gave Noah his marching orders, Noah never looked back.

We previously learned in Genesis 6:9 that Noah was physically untainted and without defect, which was remarkable in his generation. But Noah's profession of faith in God was also in perfect concert with his lifestyle. There was no hint of hypocrisy in what he said or how he lived. People knew what he believed because his life was a walking testimony. I have a cartoon imagination, and the concept of living as a walking testimony reminds me of caricatures of an old man with a waist-length white beard wearing a sandwich board with "Repent! The end is near!" painted on it. Those cartoons mock divine judgment, but that is precisely what is communicated when our faith is lived without a holy fear or reverential awe.

Second Peter 2:5 says Noah was "a preacher of righteousness." Preachers herald forth, shout, extend, promote, and cry out their messages. Noah's whole life was like a town crier or heralder shouting a clear message to those around him.

I want to give you a bit of history regarding town criers and heralds as it applies to having a bold faith. The earliest heralds were likely Spartan runners in the early Greek Empire of the fourth and fifth centuries BC. Rulers used these runners to announce news of the highest order, such as the severance of political ties, an official proclamation of war, or proposals of truce or armistice.

Later, as the Roman conquest spread throughout Europe, the position of heralds increased from disseminating information to conducting negotiations, verbalizing the demands of the realm, and announcing edicts and treaties. Even though a herald's position was official, and his words carried weight and authority, it was a dangerous occupation. If the recipients didn't like what they heard, they often killed the herald for merely delivering the news! You need to understand that in this day and age, when you are a messenger of the Lord Jesus Christ, it will cost you in some way.

Noah preached righteousness, yet there is no record of what he said. We don't know how he preached because his words weren't recorded. What we do know is that Noah was busy building an ark. Nowadays, people pile up all kinds of stuff in their yards. Can you imagine Noah's yard? I picture piles of timber and sawdust and tools everywhere. Passersby probably mocked him saying, "What are you doing there, you nutty old man?" Did Noah answer? Maybe, maybe not. One fact is certain: Every day that he worked was a proclamation of mercy before judgment.

By no means am I advocating staying silent. Judgment is coming, and we must speak when God tells us to speak. But sometimes people won't listen. It takes wisdom to know when to use words and when to let our actions do the talking. To those who are being saved, we are the fragrance of Christ, and they will receive every word as an aroma to their soul. But to others, the message of salvation is a stench.

People who disagree with you will lie about you sometimes—make sure those accusations are only lies and nothing more. They'll blame you—just make sure you're blameless. Don't defend yourself when others say or post all manner of evil things about you. God will be your defense. It is my practice to never get into a dialogue with a fool. Live out your Christianity with integrity because God wants your life to bear witness to the crucified and risen Lord.

Outside of Christ, judgment is certain. Yet in mercy, Jesus says,

"Behold, I send you out as sheep in the midst of wolves. Therefore be wise as serpents and harmless as doves" (Matthew 10:16). If a man were to write this command, he would have said, "Behold, I send you out with weapon in hand. Take control of the situation and don't take resistance lying down." But that is not Jesus' way. The implied intent and implication behind Jesus' words is that we are to be like Him in this dark world. The fact that you are a sheep shouts judgment to unbelievers. You don't need to condemn them. They are already condemned. You need to rescue them from their state of condemnation (2 Corinthians 10:4-6).

What if Noah had quietly gone about building the ark until his work was done? Are you an accountant or a doctor? A homemaker? A landscape designer or artist? What we do doesn't matter—who we are does. Our calling or vocation puts food on our table and a roof over our head, but our full-time job is being a witness for Christ. We should carry the kingdom with us in a manner that causes people to deal with the validity of our faith. One day our life's witness will end. Will we have preached mercy and judgment? We cannot have one without the other. The first is a beacon of salvation, a light to those who will hear, believe, and respond to the gospel. The other is the source of conviction and judgment upon those who refuse to hear, and to them, we are their condemnation. Both are part of our Christian life. In mercy, Jesus has sent us out among wolves, and with that sending, we express the heart of Isaiah, do we not? Will your love of God provoke you to say, "Send me"?

AN URGENT WARNING FOR TODAY

Noah wasn't the only one to witness judgment. Abraham's nephew, Lot, also had a front-row seat to God's judgment of Sodom and Gomorrah.

Sodom and Gomorrah are not simply another example of catastrophic judgment, ancient relics of the past. You can easily substitute

San Francisco and Los Angeles, or Miami and New York City in their place to see their relevance today. The destruction of Sodom and Gomorrah is a warning and challenge that all men and women today must sit up and take notice of. What God did locally in those cities, He will do again on a global scale. Isaiah 66:15-16 describes it this way:

> For behold, the LORD will come with fire
> and with His chariots, like a whirlwind,
> to render His anger with fury,
> and His rebuke with flames of fire.
> For by fire and by His sword
> the LORD will judge all flesh;
> and the slain of the LORD shall be many.

When Jesus Christ comes again in His great and terrifying second coming (Joel 2:11), there will be no place for sinners to hide, just like in the day of Sodom and Gomorrah's judgment. That God turned these cities into ashes can be visually verified by driving through the region of the Dead Sea in the southern Jordan Valley Rift. We know from the biblical account that this is the region where Sodom and Gomorrah were located. Not only is there an odd geological appearance, but geological samples from that area are unlike any other in the region. Soil samples have revealed evidence of a heat event where high temperature levels were so tremendous that it affected the geological characteristics, much like a volcanic event or when lightning strikes an area where the ground is heavy in sand content. This type of soil has often revealed a violent past in the form of fulgurite. Fulgurites are glassy tubes or crusts formed by lightning striking the ground.[2]

Englishman John Martin's famous oil painting *The Destruction of Sodom and Gomorrah* depicts fiery dark clouds encompassing cities consumed by fire from beneath and lightning from above. This depiction is not altogether the painter's idea alone. Some suggest that Sodom's fire was drawn up from the earth and rained back down with accompanying lightning, much like the action associated with volcanic activity. The Transjordan River Valley is host to ground fissures and boasts one of Earth's lengthier earthquake fault zones with combustible materials lying beneath its surface. This geological fact is a good assist for those looking for natural causes if they choose not to believe the biblical account. But the Bible says fire and brimstone hailed down from the atmosphere because God enacted judgment, and no living thing survived (Genesis 19:24-25).

We need to trust Scripture's record of how the destruction took place. And what we need to ask instead is, "Why did this happen?" If we don't answer that question, our concept of God will be distorted.

Second Peter 2:6-8 says that God made Sodom and Gomorrah "an example to those who afterward would live ungodly," while adding that He "delivered righteous Lot, who was oppressed by the filthy conduct of the wicked (for that righteous man, dwelling among them, tormented his righteous soul from day to day by seeing and hearing their lawless deeds)." The pain of past mistakes, whether ours or another's, serves as a potent teacher of what not to do. When one of our daughters was very young, she put her face close to the bottom plate of a hot iron. The plate must have looked like a mirror to her because she attempted to kiss her reflection and was nearly burned. She never did that again.

With that illustration in mind, what if I told you that aberrant, unnatural sexual activity—like that practiced in Sodom and Gomorrah—can result in a direct attack on your immune system? Or that the possibility of debilitating illnesses and premature death is a scientific fact? These are a layman's way of saying what a physician or researcher would tell someone choosing a homosexual or lesbian lifestyle.[3] If you heard that, wouldn't you stop immediately? Wouldn't you change your behavior because of the risks? Every flu season, people don masks and skip social gatherings for fear of catching the flu or common cold. How is what I've just said any different? Yet some will claim that what I've just warned about is hateful, unloving, and homophobic. But doesn't real love speak the truth? Doesn't caring for others translate into warning against harmful paths of destruction? And that violating the will of God leads to death, physical as well as spiritual death?

God, who is righteous and holy and who cares about the well-being of people, had no choice but to pronounce judgment upon Sodom and Gomorrah for the sins the people committed against themselves and one another. According to the Bible, God is long-suffering, but these people were not listening. They would not turn. God decreed a catastrophic overthrowing of those cities as an example to prevent mankind from repeating what they had done. Don't you think we'd learn? The growing trend of polyamory among young people says otherwise.

The headline of a 2019 online magazine article declared polyamory to be the next sexual frontier.[4] According to the authors, the once-taboo practice of having multiple sex partners, be it in marriage or a boyfriend-and-girlfriend relationship, is showing up in churches across the United States. The same article quotes a Christian counselor as saying, "It's only adultery or cheating if someone is kept in the dark. If you are open and honest, this can be a God-honoring relationship." That egregious and perverted statement should grieve every believer to the core.

In the years since the publication of that article, the push for mainstream polyamory has gotten stronger. Those who justify it cite Old Testament examples of men of God having concubines. In their mind, you have your wife, the mother of your children, and she's number one. When number one has a "headache," you've got number two or three to fulfill your sexual wants. And they claim you can mix it up with other sexes if you want because homosexuality wasn't what brought God's judgment upon Sodom and Gomorrah. It was the lack of hospitality shown to the visitors who came to see Lot. Those people who beat on Lot's door should have welcomed his visitors. That twisted interpretation has a big problem: There are Old and New Testament scripture passages that contradict every part of that reasoning.

Genesis 19:1-15 tells us that Lot's visitors were two angels sent to rescue him and his family before they destroyed the city. The passage also says that all the men of the city, including young boys, came pounding on Lot's door so that they might know them in a carnal or sexual manner. Because they were overly influenced by their demands of sexual gratification, they ignorantly mistook Lot's visitors to be mere mortals. Lot refused and offered his virgin daughters instead, and when the men refused Lot's offer, God instantly judged them with blindness. That should have been warning enough, but it wasn't. They wearied themselves still trying to find the door to get into Lot's house.

This was the culture Lot lived in, and it grieved him. I find it interesting that without Peter's affirmation of Lot's righteousness, we would not have known that fact. Most of us would not choose to hang out with Lot because we associate him with compromise. But before you criticize him, think carefully. If you look closely, you will discover that your environment looks just like Lot's.

Lot was exposed to wickedness every time he stepped out his door. On weekdays, when he woke up, grabbed his coffee and bagel, got on his donkey, and rode off to work, he witnessed people engaged in debauchery wherever he looked. Lot saw it all—every bit of the lawless deeds of his fellow citizens. Lot's situation is applicable in our twenty-first century because now, like then, God is shouting mercy and judgment. He is speaking to you and me because the spirit of Sodom and Gomorrah never left. It is still here. And it is fueled by dark, unseen spirit forces rampant in our world today.

As Christians, we are no longer held captive to fleshly demands, and when the Holy Spirit reminds us of Sodom and Gomorrah in Scripture, He does so to highlight that difference unapologetically. We were once as they were but are no longer. "You were once darkness, but now you are light in the Lord. Walk as children of light" (Ephesians 5:8).

The wording "you were once darkness" is not a grammatical error. The Holy Spirit didn't forget to insert the word "in" between "once" and "darkness." Ephesians 5:8 means that darkness emanated from our lives—we were the darkness! Sinning came easy. We didn't need anyone's coaching. We were the ones who used other people. We were those who wounded and injured others.

Our flesh screamed and yelled constantly, "I want, I want, I want." The flesh wanted appeasement. Whether it was one more drink, a casual flirtation, the click of the "buy now" button, or a myriad of desires, it had to have its way. "Nothing rough or uncomfortable. I want it all smooth and easy. I want it nice." That, my friend, is the voice of the flesh, and until you bring those desires into subjection to God's Word and His will, your flesh will win those battles. You will remain in a spiritual coma of sorts. But once you come to grips with the magnitude of your sins and realize *I am a rotten wretch whom God delivered from darkness and set in the light,* only then will you love Him as you ought. Jesus said that it is those kinds of people who will love much (Luke 7:47) and act on that love.

When we're tempted to love other things more than we love the Lord, we must resist! First John 2:15 commands, "Do not love the world or the things in the world. If anyone loves the world, the love of the Father is not in him." There is little room for the love of God when there is too much love of the world in your heart.

BE GOD'S MESSENGER OF MERCY AND GRACE

Lover of God, carry heaven's influence to all the places you traffic. The closing days of this world are drawing near. Judgment is on the horizon. It is our responsibility to warn others of the smoke and fire. Some will refuse to be saved, but there might be one or five or ten who say, "Yes, Lord. I repent. I've had enough. I am Yours."

Some time ago, I gave a message in which I mentioned the topics we've covered in this chapter, and a woman was watching on television. Months later, she decided to visit the church and met me in the foyer. She said it was as if a lightning bolt shot from the screen into her heart and convicted her. She had been living a particular lifestyle, but in that instant became a new creation in Christ just as 2 Corinthians 5:17 promises. Now she is reading her Bible, making new friends, and living a new life. Her whole world is brand new!

Lover of God, carry heaven's
influence to all the places you traffic.

The parallels between the ancient world and ours are concerning and encouraging: concerning because the spirit and sins of Sodom and Gomorrah are more prevalent than ever—man's wickedness is great, judgment is guaranteed, and people's souls are at stake. Yet encouraging because though our hearts grieve over our brothers, sisters, children, and friends trapped by the seduction of this world, God's hand of mercy remains outstretched. May we be used as instruments of His grace to rescue them.

CHAPTER 10

THE FALSE AND THE TRUE

The signs are everywhere. Posted outside of residences and businesses alike are announcements that a security service protects the premises. One of the unfortunate realities of our world is rising lawlessness, which makes people desperate for safety from the outside world. Yet the one place where they should be safe—God's house—is not always the case.

Jesus said, "I am the door. If anyone enters by Me, he will be saved, and will go in and out and find pasture. The thief does not come except to steal, and to kill, and to destroy" (John 10:9-10). Spiritual thieves masquerading as Christians are happy to rob you of your faith, steal your liberty in Christ, and lie about it in the process. Unfortunately, most of us will be taken advantage of at least once in our lifetime, but no deception is more dangerous or hurtful than when it's directed at spiritual things and empowered by Satan.

The last several chapters have focused primarily on the spiritual charlatans associated with the last days. We've seen how the dynamics of spiritual truths and falsehoods are played out in the physical realm. Yet, because we traffic in the material world, we quickly forget how connected we are with the spiritual battle between darkness and light.

We would do well to remember three areas vulnerable to demonic attack. The first is religion. Satan loves to infiltrate religious settings in his quest to deceive. But if someone isn't interested in religion, that's okay. He has another line of attack—politics. Globally, nations are cracking under the strain of recent events, and in response, leaders are ushering in ideologies promising a collective utopia that human nature renders impossible. Yet citizens looking to replace God with government as the provider of every need are falling for this deception wholesale. And then there are the dark powers present in the realm of business.

Satan makes it a point to move among the movers and shakers of the business world. If you have any doubts, look at companies like Google, Microsoft, and Amazon. Dig into the extent of their individual holdings, some of which might surprise you. Those three giants are hard at work to provide everything required for a community or nation to function—making other options unnecessary. For example, Jeff Bezos envisions Amazon becoming embedded in a customer's lifestyle. His goal is making Amazon a daily habit.[1] Small and mid-sized businesses are closing at breakneck speed because they can't compete with these types of global conglomerates. All of which fits into a last-days scenario.

Why is this happening? Control. A famous quote taken from a letter that English historian Lord Acton wrote to Bishop Creighton in 1887 sums it up perfectly. Acton believed the same moral standards should be applied to all men—political and religious leaders alike—because "power tends to corrupt and absolute power corrupts absolutely."[2] Power and corruption often go hand in hand, and Satan knows this.

EMPTY AND DRY

The advances of satanic influence in government and industry are indisputable, but the devil's most virulent attacks are aimed at weakening the church. In writing to the believers in Corinth, the apostle Paul warned,

> False apostles, deceitful workers, transforming themselves into apostles of Christ. And no wonder! For Satan himself transforms himself into an angel of light. Therefore it is no great thing if his ministers also transform themselves into ministers of righteousness, whose end will be according to their works (2 Corinthians 11:13-15).

False apostles, doing false ministry, in what are no doubt false churches, are those who promise much but offer nothing. These types of leaders are "wells without water, clouds carried by a tempest" (2 Peter 2:17). To the early Christians, this language was graphic. For us to grasp the full meaning today, we need to dig a little deeper (pun intended).

The necessity of a well implies thirst. For most of us, this is hard to relate to because quenching our thirst usually involves grabbing a glass and turning on the kitchen tap to fill it with water. But imagine traveling through the United States's driest place, California's Death Valley, and running out of water. If that happened, you would go hunting for a well, and when you found one, you'd drop a rock down the well and listen. What would you listen for? A splash. The sound you don't want to hear is the tell-tale sign of an empty well—silence; the same response people looking for refreshment from false teachers get. When you hang around those types of waterless wells long enough, you will begin to think that they define what a well should be—dry with nothing in it except a sandy bottom, incapable of offering refreshment. But without spiritual water there is no vitality, which equals dead Christianity.

So, the well is dry, and you are still thirsty. Now what do you hope for? Rain. But Jude 1:12 tells us that these false teachers can't supply that either because they are like clouds driven by the wind—they're just passing through.

Clouds are amazing, and I happen to love them. I can name the various types, what is happening inside them, which ones are safe to fly through, and those to avoid. But the contrast between a well and a cloud is striking. A well can quickly run out of water because it is only a hole dug into stony ground. But a cloud consists of water. Meteorologists say that depending on the size and type, a cloud can hold tons of water—water that is meant to replenish and refresh.

The sight of clouds assumes a blessing is in store—water is on the way. Nothing is worse than watching a cloud pass overhead during a drought, only for it to give nothing. Likewise, you can be thirsty and go looking for hope from a church or ministry, but if the message it proclaims lacks spiritual truth and substance, there is no watering of your soul. You'll walk out the door just as parched as when you entered and worse off because you are less hopeful for the experience. And herein is a warning: False teachers are like wind-driven storm clouds that withhold refreshment. They know the truth, but they refuse to dispense it. Believer beware!

LEGALISTIC HYPOCRITES

Spiritual dryness often manifests itself in a lethargic, indifferent faith. But know this: God wants you to experience something better, deeper, and far more effective. That may mean taking the difficult yet bold step of finding a new church or leaving your family's lifelong denomination. But I urge you, don't settle for a blasé, safe faith simply because it's easier!

Today, many churches are filled with people who accept spiritual dryness as normal, never realizing they need the life-giving water of the gospel and true spirituality. Sadly, many of them have been "churched" their whole lives. The same was true in Jesus' day.

When a large crowd gathered to hear Jesus teach, He warned, "Beware of the leaven of the Pharisees" (Luke 12:1). The disciples heard this and likely thought, *We should have brought a couple of loaves of bread along.* Jesus had to tell them, "I am not talking about bread but their hypocritical doctrine." The Pharisees used the law to keep people bound in the practice of adhering to the law. But wait! Isn't the law good? Oh, yes. The law is beyond good. It is perfect.

The Ten Commandments are perfect, and when used rightly, can make a person aware of their sin and their need for Jesus Christ as Savior. But the requirements of the Ten Commandments cannot be kept. Religion and morality are also fine if focused correctly, but neither can do anything about your eternal soul. What is required is an actual, intimate relationship with God.

The Pharisees told people, "Get circumcised, keep our rules and regulations, obey the law of Moses, and you'll make it to heaven." The only problem is that nobody can do all those things. The person who looks at the law and says, "I'm good. I'm okay," only does so by measuring themselves horizontally against others, not vertically against the holiness of God.

Pharisaical doctrine leads to legalism, which the Bible condemns. "By the works of the law no flesh shall be justified" (Galatians 2:16). Legalism always hurts, leaves its practitioners wounded, and crushes the soul and spirit. Anyone who promotes it can never refresh you because they always have one more thing for you to do, one more load for you to bear.

As religious leaders, the Pharisees laid heavy burdens on people's shoulders that they couldn't keep themselves (Matthew 23:3-4). More than once, Jesus called them hypocrites for that reason. Whether they were leaders or everyday people, the Jews could not keep the law. Jeremiah 31:31-33 proves it.

> Behold, the days are coming, says the LORD, when I will make a new covenant with the house of Israel and with the house of Judah—not according to the covenant that I made with their fathers in the day that I took them by the hand to lead them out of the land of Egypt, My covenant which they broke, though I was a husband to them, says the LORD. But this is the covenant that I will make with the house of Israel after those days, says the LORD: I will put My law in their minds, and write it on their hearts; and I will be their God, and they shall be My people.

Atop Mount Sinai, God gave Moses the Ten Commandments for His people. But when Moses came down the mountain, Joshua met him, saying that there was a sound of war in the camp. Moses said, "No, that isn't war. They're partying." In Moses' absence, the people replaced their worship of the living God with the worship of a molded calf (Exodus 32:8-10, 15-18).

Right from the beginning, the people of Israel broke their covenant with the Lord, even though He was a husband to them. But they were not left without hope. God promised to make a new covenant with them, which is remarkable because that promise appears throughout the Bible and applies to Israel first *and* then to the Gentiles. It's universal. "I will put My law in their minds and write it on their hearts; and I will be their God, and they will be My people" is the born-again experience. And when—not if—you break a commandment, you go straight to Christ and say, "Lord, I shouldn't have done this thing or had that thought."

In Matthew 5:28, Jesus made the point that the law can be broken in the heart and mind, even when the sinful desire hasn't been lived out. Keeping the law, whether externally or internally, is impossible, and therefore, cannot save anyone, including Jews. This makes it hard to understand why there is debate in religious circles about how Jews are saved. It is mystifying, because Jesus' words to Nicodemus, a Jew, were unequivocal: "Most assuredly, I say to you, unless one is born again, he cannot see the kingdom of God" (John 3:3).

As a Pharisee, Nicodemus was a moral man who tithed and kept all the law's rules and regulations. But none of that mattered. There isn't one way of salvation for Jews and another for Gentiles. We all come to Christ the same way. We must stand strong against anyone who teaches otherwise.

Sometimes a picture really is worth a thousand words, and that is certainly true of a mural I saw depicting a biblical commentary from one of Christianity's great reformers. The mural is done in black and white pencil, and shows a wretched sinner cowering, wide-eyed and terrified. Above him stands the fiery-eyed lawgiver, Moses, with the Ten Commandments in hand, ready to crush the man. But between the law and the man stands Jesus with back bent and nail-pierced hands reaching out to shield the sinner from the blow that fell on Him instead. Jesus' death fulfilled the law so that sinners could go free.

Salvation comes through what Christ did on the cross, and through this, the Spirit of truth "dwells with you and will be in you" (John 14:17). This is how personal our God is. But cults and false teachers will never teach you this. They want you to remain in constant dependence upon them or their movement or denomination. In their desire for control, many will institute a Nicolaitan type of leadership that knowingly robs you of real faith, saving faith, a bold faith.

What is the antidote to legalism? I believe it's found in 2 Timothy 3:16: "All Scripture is given by inspiration of God, and is profitable for doctrine, for reproof, for correction, for instruction in righteousness." All Scripture means the Bible from cover to cover—the full counsel of God. The full counsel of God leads us to repentance, corrects our thinking, and affects our behavior. It shows us God's will for our lives and the right way to do it. If we focused on that one verse alone, all our lives would do well.

Christianity isn't something you conjure up or work hard at—God does it. He brings you into His family, sovereignly takes over your life, turns you around, and sends you down the mountain, as it were, to a lost world.

MASTERS OF ENSLAVEMENT

Regardless of their pedigree or status in life, people long for liberty. One of the great crimes Satan perpetrates against humanity is convincing individuals that religion takes away a person's freedom. Legalistic religion is certainly guilty as charged, but some pulpits offer a form of liberty that is, in reality, slavery.

Skilled at tempting and masters in the art of enslavement, false teachers promise liberty, but what they're offering becomes bondage for the takers—"for whom a person is overcome, by him also he is brought into bondage" (2 Peter 2:19). I once read that this pictures a man in a sinkhole. He calls out to you, but instead of taking ahold of the rope you throw him, he reaches out and grabs you, pulling you into his pit of corruption. The many facets of bondage are vast, but if you can imagine something, a false teacher can repackage that thing and make it part of their religious indoctrination.

The irony of deceptive liberty is that it can lead to enslavement of mind or body, or both. I've heard from parents whose children moved out of the family home, went to college, or set out to establish their place in the world, and along the way, found a church to attend. You hear that and think, *Great!* But then they explain that their son or daughter never drank alcohol, cursed, or dabbled in other vices. Yet after a few weeks of attending this new church, they were celebrating carnality rather than enjoying the freedom that comes from a transformative faith. The kids say, "I didn't know this before, but I get to drink. I get to curse. I have liberty in Christ to do as I please." The truth is, biblical liberty is the power to not do the things the world does. It's not what we are free to do, but what we are free not to do that matters.

The sad truth about following in the footsteps of a false teacher's corrupt liberty is that people do it willingly. One day, a sinful idea enters their mind, and they entertain it until the desire starts taking root. They say to themselves, *I'm intrigued by what I see so-and-so doing. There doesn't seem to be any consequences. It must be sort of okay. I'm going to dabble just a little bit in this one area.* They commit the first act, whatever it is, and they know they've crossed the line. Red lights are going off, alarms are screaming, their conscience is convicted, and they promise themselves, *I'll never do that again!* Until next week. They do it a second time and feel terrible, but even though they know it's not right, they begin rationalizing their actions. They are enjoying themselves, so why stop? By the third, fourth, or fifteenth time, they don't feel bad at all. Why? Because their heart has hardened to the things of God.

To do this is like stepping into wet concrete. A person sinks up to their ankles, and a godly friend warns, "Get out," but unexpectedly, the person likes the sensation of wet cement. So, the compromiser either ignores the friend or tells him to mind his own business. Initially the person can move around and talk to others who warn, "You better get out, and quick!" But because the person is bent on resisting and acting like everything is good, even normal, he stays until the cement hardens, making it impossible to move. He has been lied to—conditioned by a culture energized to tempt, deceive, and enslave—and now, he can't free himself.

Don't let that scenario be true of you. A friend once made a statement that I've never forgotten. He said, "Satan is a gradualist."

I caution you to resist the allurements of false liberty because it is an anathema to God when the church contradicts His Word in its agreement with the world. Dangerous teachers have labeled portions of Scripture unnecessarily restrictive in their quest to be seen as nonjudgmental. Some, not unlike the young people mentioned earlier, want to make passages like 1 Corinthians 6:9-10 null and void. "Do you not know that the unrighteous will not inherit the kingdom of God? Do not be deceived. Neither fornicators, nor idolaters, nor adulterers, nor homosexuals, nor sodomites, nor thieves, nor covetous, nor drunkards, nor revilers, nor extortioners will inherit the kingdom of God." The Bible says don't be deceived into thinking you are heaven bound if you practice any of these things. This is not true faith.

I want to reemphasize what I said in a previous chapter. Many false teachers can recite the gospel, preach it, write books about it, and share it—yet none of the effects of the gospel are present in their lives. Even though they manage some form of outward reformation, they are never inwardly renewed. Instead, they return to their previous sins only to become "entangled in them and overcome, the latter end is worse for them than the beginning" (2 Peter 2:20).

The word translated "entangled" is a first-century Greek word meaning interwoven, much like the woven and knotted gladiator's net used by the Roman retiarius or "net man." Picture two men fighting in an arena. One guy is bigger, stronger, and armed with better swords, but the other has a weighted net along with his trident and dagger. If the retiarius employs the gladiatorial net against his adversary by throwing it over him, his opponent is entangled with no hope of escape—his death is assured. The fate of false teachers is distressing, but it should also serve as a graphic warning.

JUSTICE IS COMING!

Being taken advantage of through empty words and false promises is painful, but when it's done under religious trappings, the damage can be devastating. Someone you relied on for spiritual guidance broke your trust, and it's natural for you to want justice and want it now. Yet have you noticed how human justice is often terribly flawed? How it sometimes fails to render true justice? Believer, based on Scripture, patience is in order.

The Bible says without apology that a terrible end is awaiting false teachers. Be glad your name is written in the Lamb's Book of Life because theirs is not—theirs appears in hell's ledger! Divine, pure, holy, perfect, and exacting justice is coming. God says, "Just wait. I have judged them, and herein is justice." He reserves for them "the blackness of darkness forever" (2 Peter 2:17).

Regarding God's ultimate judgment, one of the hardest things to do in life is wait. But one day, all wrongs will be made right. When I think about the difficulty of waiting for justice, I am reminded of the words of a song lifted from the Old Testament book of Joel. Americans will recognize it as "The Battle Hymn of the Republic."

> Mine eyes have seen the glory of the coming of the Lord;
> He is trampling out the vintage where the grapes
> of wrath are stored;
> He hath loosed the fateful lightning of His terrible
> swift sword:
> His truth is marching on.
>
> I have seen Him in the watch-fires of a hundred circling camps,
> They have builded Him an altar in the evening dews and damps;
> I can read His righteous sentence by the dim and flaring lamps:
> His day is marching on.
>
> I have read a fiery gospel writ in burnished rows of steel:
> "As ye deal with My contemners, so with you
> My grace shall deal;
> Let the Hero, born of woman, crush the serpent
> with his heel,
> Since God is marching on."

> He has sounded forth the trumpet that shall never
>   call retreat;
> He is sifting out the hearts of men before His
>   judgment-seat;
> Oh, be swift, my soul, to answer Him! Be jubilant, my feet!
> Our God is marching on.
>
> In the beauty of the lilies Christ was born across the sea,
> With a glory in His bosom that transfigures you and me.
> As He died to make men holy, let us die to make men free,
> While God is marching on.[3]

The words "His truth is marching on" and "His day is marching on" remind us that all those who are opposed to God will not get away with what they're doing. Jesus Christ is coming! We must be ready. And to be ready, we must nurture and develop a strong faith.

STAND, PERSEVERE, AND ADVANCE

The thought of Christ's glorious return should galvanize the faith of believers, but tragically, we are witnessing massive apostasy instead. The church no longer knows what it is supposed to stand for or has simply given up. In the face of legalism and false liberty, we must stand fast in the liberty by which Christ has made us free and refuse to be entangled again with a yoke of bondage (Galatians 5:1). But can you say today that you are free? Before you answer, let me explain what freedom means.

Our Christian freedom is synonymous with what God has done and is doing in our lives. He set us free from sin and death, and now, by the power of the Holy Spirit, He is leading and directing us. Likewise, true liberty unfetters us from anything holding us back from fully walking in the direction God intends. It is freedom from the paralyzing fear of people and circumstances.

Christian liberty means that you are a citizen of a heavenly country whose king is God Almighty. I love that! This is not the liberty to sin, act up, be silly or weird, but the liberty to advance the kingdom of God. True freedom is active. It's not a leisurely pastime.

Jesus Christ is coming! We must be ready. And to be ready, we must nurture and develop a strong faith.

To stand fast in Christ's liberty is to have your feet firmly fixed, yet with the intent of persevering and advancing. It's like the stance a batter takes in a baseball game. His feet are firmly planted at home base, but his eyes are on the ball and he's ready to swing with all his might, and then run!

Perhaps you are not truly free, and there is only the slightest sliver remaining of your relationship with Jesus. God is calling you to repent—that is, to stop doing what you are doing and start doing as Scripture commands—and then strengthen what remains (Revelation 3:2). Endeavor to not trample the doctrines of God or sacrifice of Christ—His cross, blood, and resurrection—underfoot by the weight of your lifestyle. Do away with any hypocrisy in your life because, as we've learned, believing that you can fool God is futile.

Have you been playing games with God? Decide to start over. Go back in your heart to that place where you were first illuminated by the Spirit and met Christ, and in that remembrance, determine to respond to His love by persevering in the present.

We must go beyond superficiality—beyond the manufactured veneer that says everything is fine and good all the time. It discourages those going through tough times by making them believe God cannot use them. Not true! Remember, Satan thrives on making people think that way. He is an excellent devil—the best ever—who whispers what a bad Christian you are. He's the first to remind you how little you're praying and how little Bible reading you do. Satan is the first to say, "Didn't you hear the pastor? You're supposed to share the Lord. How many people have you led to Christ this week?" But let me encourage you: We all need to resist Satan because he is an equal-opportunity liar.

As the founding and senior pastor of the same church for some 35 years and counting, I rarely share personal struggles, but in this case, I hope doing so will provide an encouraging perspective.

A few years ago, I struggled with insomnia so badly that I attempted to resign several times, as it had reached a critical state. When you have severe insomnia, you can't read because your eyes burn so badly, your brain hurts, and you can't remember a thing. I missed two-and-a-half months of pulpit time because I could barely put one foot in front of the other.

I eventually came under the care of one of the top sleep specialists in America, but to no avail. After some time he said, "I am unable to determine the cause of your insomnia." As soon as I heard those words, I was filled with hope because I knew I was facing a spiritual battle. But that wasn't the end of it.

The insomnia continued for two-and-a-half years, leaving me gutted. There were several Sundays when I couldn't remember how I got home from church. Once, when I didn't sleep for 72 hours, I called a Navy Seal friend and asked him, "How do you endure not sleeping for extended periods? I am sick to my stomach." His answer: "We're sick for about three days after that kind of experience. But here's the thing: I was twenty-four years old and you're sixty-something. I'm not sure how to help you."

Throughout that tough period, I lived and pastored through the prayers of others and the faithfulness of my wife's ministry to me. A couple of years later, the COVID pandemic hit, and church closure edicts were issued statewide. But we followed Jesus' promise that He had set before us an open door (Revelation 3:8).

No man had the authority to shut the doors of Jesus' church, and we took the bold step of reopening on May 31, 2020, despite intense opposition. Consequently, our congregation exploded in the best of ways. Countless people came to faith in Christ, many believers rededicated their lives, and over 3,000 people of all ages were baptized during that time! It was the COVID Revival!

As a church family, we simply lived out biblical Christianity by confronting those in the wrong and standing for what was God-honoring. We watched in amazement as the Lord worked in ways none of us could have imagined—and He is still at work to this day.

Why was I afflicted with sleeplessness to the point of breaking? Those years were in exact accordance with Romans 8:28: "We know that all things work together for good to those who love God, to those who are the called according to His purpose." In 2 Corinthians, the apostle Paul talks about how "all things" play into our lives and ministry, and I appreciate that he doesn't reveal the exact nature of his trials. All who are suffering can relate: "We were burdened beyond measure, above strength, so that we despaired even of life. Yes, we had the sentence of death in ourselves, that we should not trust in ourselves but in God who raises the dead" (2 Corinthians 1:8-9). Commenting on verse 9, Alan Redpath wrote, "This ministry is a ministry of the Holy Spirit alone, and He cannot work where there is self-confidence."[4] And to that, I say, "Amen!"

In hindsight, I believe God stripped me of myself in preparation for what He knew was about to transpire. None of me could be left so that it would be evident the work was His, and all praise belonged to Him alone.

Have you convinced yourself, *If only my job, my health, or my situation were different, then I would do x, y, or z?* Stop thinking that way! No one is exempt from hardship, and in today's cultural climate, persecution and suffering are inevitable as we continue to stand for righteousness. It is time we adopted Paul's mindset:

> Not that I have already attained, or am already perfected; but I press on, that I may lay hold of that for which Christ Jesus has also laid hold of me. Brethren, I do not count myself to have apprehended; but one thing I do, forgetting those things which are behind and reaching forward to those things which are ahead, I press toward the goal for the prize of the upward call of God in Christ Jesus (Philippians 3:12-14).

Christian, do everything within your power to stand in God's Word and determine to go forward with full force. When we look forward and upward to the coming of Christ, the future looks brighter than the noonday sun. And this is the bedrock of our confidence: Jesus is coming soon!

PART 3

GOING PUBLIC

CHAPTER 11

WHAT ARE YOU WAITING FOR?

Can you feel it? Do you sense that something big is about to happen? And by big, I mean an event or events affecting people on a global scale. I am convinced that Spirit-filled believers are detecting what the Puritans called the *quickening*. To quicken is to bring to life, accelerate, or incite. Pregnant women experience quickening with a baby's first movements, and more importantly, the term also describes an advanced stage of pregnancy that alerts the mother that her long-awaited day is near—even imminent.

The Bible says that people are spiritually quickened or made alive when they are born again and will be physically quickened at the resurrection. Now, ask yourself: "Are there signs that events are accelerating before us, moving us toward the end of the age? Is there a tension that seems to indicate God is about to intervene in our lives?" I would say yes! This quickening is a reminder to the church of what is soon to come. And it is a tremendous time to be alive.

It is true that anti-Christian sentiment is rising—as we should expect—because believing in Jesus Christ divides. I can say any name at any given time, anywhere, and it's not a problem. Yet division is guaranteed when anyone mentions the name of Jesus Christ outside the walls of a church. If believing in Jesus is divisive, believing in the rapture and its imminency creates an even greater divide. How so? It was Jesus Himself who introduced the doctrine of the rapture in John 14:1-3.

The Bible tells us that the rapture will separate believers from nonbelievers. Suddenly, without notice or any prerequisite, believers will instantly vanish, being transformed and translated into the spirit realm. Though believers are awaiting that day, many others are not. Sadly, husbands, wives, family, and friends who do not know the Lord will not experience this blessed hope. Many even mock the rapture as a fairy tale, the proverbial pie in the sky, or escapism. But being raptured is not without precedent. It has happened before.

The Old Testament saint Enoch "walked with God; and he was not, for God took him" (Genesis 5:24). Hebrews 11:5 elaborates, "By faith Enoch was taken away so that he did not see death, 'and was not found, because God had taken him'; for before he was taken he had this testimony, that he pleased God."

The prophet Elijah left earth without seeing death when "suddenly a chariot of fire appeared with horses of fire and separated the two of them; and Elijah went up by a whirlwind into heaven" (2 Kings 2:11).

I want to stress that the pulpit ministry of the church today needs to sound a clear note of hope regarding the rapture. It is not silly to preach that believers can have hope amidst persecution or in the moment of devastation or disease. God's pulpits should never be places of weakness, gloom, apathy, or fear. Christians need to stop being constantly afraid because it accomplishes nothing except to stop us dead in our tracks. Fear never makes anything better and often serves to make situations worse. Yet when we arm ourselves with the hope of the rapture, we are inspired to look heavenward and confidently keep moving forward in this world, resulting in a stronger faith.

Pulpits ought to be ablaze with the truth that points all Christians to the blessed hope (Titus 2:13). We should be excited at the prospect of Christ gathering His people to Himself and continue to soldier on until He comes. This is not a pipe dream. The doctrine of imminency teaches that the rapture could happen at any moment (1 Thessalonians 5:6; Hebrews 9:28). I pray, "Dear Lord, come now!"

IS THE RAPTURE BIBLICAL?

Christians believe in the rapture because it is clearly taught in the Bible. It is a biblical doctrine. Some challenge that statement because the word *rapture* doesn't appear in our English Bibles, but it does appear in the Latin Bible as *rapturo*. To be raptured is to be "caught up or pulled up suddenly." Remember, Jesus introduced the doctrine of the rapture in John 14:1-3, when He said:

> Let not your heart be troubled; you believe in God, believe also in Me. In My Father's house are many mansions; if it were not so, I would have told you. I go to prepare a place for you. And if I go and prepare a place for you, I will come again and receive you to Myself; that where I am, there you may be also.

To skeptics who doubt the veracity of the rapture, I have a couple of questions. Following His resurrection, did Jesus ascend to heaven? Yes, He did. According to Acts 1:9, the disciples watched as He was taken up. So, is Jesus in heaven right now? Yes, He is. And did Jesus say He was going to prepare a place for us and come back just long enough to pick us up and take us back to where He is? Yes, He did, in John 14:2-3. I submit to you that the way Jesus will accomplish this is through the rapture.

Every Bible-believing Christian familiar with Scripture understands that the rapture is a fact. They may disagree on the timing of it—before, during, or after the seven-year tribulation period—and that is okay with me. Believers can disagree on timing, but we cannot say, "There is no rapture." To say that would mean deleting John 14:1-3 and numerous other passages right out of the Bible.

When God's Word speaks of the coming separation of the righteous from the unrighteous, it doesn't leave us in the dark as to how it will happen. Paul wrote to the Corinthian believers,

> Behold, I tell you a mystery: We shall not all sleep, but we shall all be changed—in a moment, in the twinkling of an eye, at the last trumpet. For the trumpet will sound, and the dead will be raised incorruptible, and we shall be changed. For this corruptible must put on incorruption, and this mortal must put on immortality (1 Corinthians 15:51-53).

Paul wasn't making up some fantastic story when he said this was a mystery. The word "mystery" here means it's an eternal truth that has now been made known. Paul was saying, "I'm telling you something that has always been true but is now being revealed openly." And when he used the term "sleep" in verse 51, he did so as an affectionate way of referring to a believer who has died. Allow me to paraphrase these verses a bit for clarity's sake: "We shall not all die, but we shall be changed in a moment, in the twinkling of an eye at the last trumpet. For the trumpet will sound, and the dead in Christ will be raised incorruptible."

It is interesting to note that Paul also taught the Thessalonian believers about the rapture. He was with them for only three or four weeks, so time was of the essence in teaching them the essential doctrines of the faith—including the doctrine of the rapture. In fact, it was so important to Paul that when he wrote to those believers later, he discussed the rapture five times.

> Wait for His Son from heaven, whom He raised from the dead, even Jesus who delivers us from the wrath to come (1 Thessalonians 1:10).
>
> What is our hope, or joy, or crown of rejoicing? Is it not even you in the presence of our Lord Jesus Christ at His coming? (1 Thessalonians 2:19).
>
> ...so that He may establish your hearts blameless in holiness before our God and Father at the coming of our Lord Jesus Christ with all His saints (1 Thessalonians 3:13).
>
> If we believe that Jesus died and rose again, even so God will bring with Him those who sleep in Jesus (1 Thessalonians 4:14).
>
> God did not appoint us to wrath, but to obtain salvation through our Lord Jesus Christ (1 Thessalonians 5:9).

Paul understood the rapture to be imminent, meaning there is nothing more that needs to be fulfilled in biblical prophecy before this event occurs. This exciting news would have thrilled the hearts of the Thessalonians, as it should for us today. Wherever you are right now, can you take a moment to say, "Thank You, God, for this ever-present blessed hope!"

WHAT ABOUT BELIEVERS WHO DIE BEFORE THE RAPTURE?

Perhaps a believing friend or relative has already died and you are concerned about how the rapture relates to them. You are not alone in your concern. The Thessalonian believers questioned Paul on this very topic, and to calm their fears and comfort their hearts, he wrote:

> If we believe that Jesus died and rose again, even so God will bring with Him those who sleep in Jesus. For this we say to you by the word of the Lord, that we who are alive and remain until the coming of the Lord will by no means precede those who are asleep. For the Lord Himself will descend from heaven with a shout, with the voice of an archangel, and with the trumpet of God. And the dead in Christ will rise first. Then we who are alive and remain shall be caught up together with them in the clouds to meet the Lord in the air. And thus we shall always be with the Lord. Therefore comfort one another with these words (1 Thessalonians 4:14-18).

Prior to the rapture, when a believer dies, their body is buried or cremated, and their spirit goes to be with the Lord—to be "absent from the body...[is] to be present with the Lord" (2 Corinthians 5:8). When Jesus comes for His church, He will raise up those dead bodies and give them brand-new resurrected bodies. Then we who are alive and remain will be caught up. "Caught up" is translated from the Greek word *harpazo*, which was translated *rapturo* in the Latin Bible. "And thus we shall always be with the Lord. Therefore comfort one another with these words" (verses 17-18). Does someone you know need comfort? Remind them Christ is coming back! But before you do, I urge you to read the fine print in verse 14 because it is very important. Not everyone benefits from the crucifixion and resurrection of Christ.

God's great gift to mankind was manifested in Jesus because God the Father "so loved the world that He gave"—gifted the world—"His only-begotten Son, that whosoever believes in Him should not perish but have eternal life" (John 3:16). A gift is meant to be received, but it cannot be received unless the recipient chooses to accept it. It is tragic when gifts are rejected with the words "return to sender." Refusing an extravagant gift from someone who cares deeply about you is a heartbreaking form of rejection. Yet, people do that with the gospel. The gospel goes out, and they say, "I don't want or need it." But believe me, when the day of separation comes, you will want to have received the gift of salvation through Christ. He is your passport to heaven.

THE RAPTURE ASSURES DELIVERANCE

If I asked you which nation is the star, so to speak, of the entire Bible, what would you say? What nation has the sweet distinction of being the apple of God's eye (Zechariah 2:8)? You would have to say Israel. And yet, Israel regularly rejected God's faithfulness, love, and kindness despite His blessings upon her. So, the fact that God says He will save Israel in the end is amazing (Zechariah 12:10; Romans 11:26; Revelation 7–9). I have Canadian friends who are dear to my heart, but there is no biblical promise that Canada will be saved in the end. As nations go, there is no promise that America, Sweden, France, nor Australia will be saved in the end. Israel is the only nation that God promises will be saved through the time of great difficulty yet to come—a time that Jeremiah 30:7 calls "Jacob's trouble"—the seven-year tribulation.

To say that Israel's future will be challenging is an understatement. As a nation, the people will continue to reject Christ, and in those days of deception, most of Israel will accept the false peace and false prosperity the Antichrist promises. Where are we in the last days' timeline? We cannot pinpoint where we are for sure, but we know these two things: We are 2,000 years closer, and while there has been global upheaval in the past, what we see today is different.

Times are tough, but this is not the tribulation period, contrary to some misinformed souls you read online. What is one indicator of that? God promised to take Israel through the tribulation period, but not the church, because believers will already be raptured to be with Christ—and yet, for now, here we are. "Watch therefore, and pray always that you may be counted worthy to escape all these things that will come to pass, and to stand before the Son of Man" (Luke 21:26).

Although Israel and the church are two separate dispensations and distinct entities, I want to point you to an Old Testament passage that concerns both—Isaiah 26:19-20. While these verses apply to Israel, it cannot be denied that its theology mirrors that of the New Testament saints' deliverance from God's coming wrath. Verse 19 says, "Your dead shall live; together with my dead body they shall arise." Think of Christ's resurrection. "Awake and sing, you who dwell in dust." Think of those who have died in Christ—their bodies have turned to dust. "For your dew is like the dew of herbs." What do you see when the sun first comes up? Droplets of water upon plant leaves and petals. If you patiently sit and watch, these droplets will become smaller and smaller as evaporation eventually receives them back up into the atmosphere. Verse 19 says, "And the earth shall cast out the dead." That sounds a lot like 1 Thessalonians 4:16: "The dead in Christ will rise first."

Verse 20 continues, "Come, my people, enter your chambers, and shut your doors behind you; hide yourself, as it were, for a little moment, until the indignation is past." What indignation is Isaiah speaking of? "For behold, the LORD comes out of His place to punish *the inhabitants of the earth* for their iniquity" (verse 21). The wrath of God levied against a Christ-rejecting world will be of no consequence to the church He has safely tucked away.

Foundational to the rapture is 2 Peter 2:9: "The Lord knows how to deliver the godly out of temptations and to reserve the unjust under punishment for the day of judgment." Christians will never see a day of judgment from the wrath of God. Jesus said so. "Most assuredly, I say to you, he who hears My word and believes in Him who sent Me has everlasting life, and shall not come into judgment, but has passed from death into life" (John 5:24). Because of Jesus, you and I will never suffer the wrath of God, ever.

How can we be so sure? Revelation 2–4 substantiates that assertion perfectly. Jesus speaks to the seven churches in chapters 2–3, but in chapter 4, John, the book's writer, is taken up to heaven, and what he sees is exciting!

> After these things I looked, and behold, a door standing open in heaven. And the first voice which I heard was like a trumpet speaking with me, saying, "Come up here, and I will show you things which must take place after this." Immediately I was in the Spirit; and behold, a throne set in heaven, and One sat on the throne. And He who sat there was like a jasper and a sardius stone in appearance; and there was a rainbow around the throne, in appearance like an emerald (Revelation 4:1-3).

I do not know how it is possible for a rainbow's coloration to appear as an emerald. Perhaps the stones on earth are only a poor facsimile of heaven's precious gems. Truly, this is beyond our human comprehension, and that's okay. We'll understand that and more when we get there. But let's continue:

> Around the throne were twenty-four thrones, and on the thrones I saw twenty-four elders sitting, clothed in white robes; and they had crowns of gold on their heads. And from the throne proceeded lightnings, thunderings, and voices. Seven lamps of fire were burning before the throne, which are the seven Spirits of God.

> Before the throne there was a sea of glass, like crystal. And in the midst of the throne, and around the throne, were four living creatures full of eyes in front and in back. The first living creature was like a lion, the second living creature like a calf, the third living creature had a face like a man, and the fourth living creature was like a flying eagle. The four living creatures, each having six wings, were full of eyes around and within. And they do not rest day or night, saying:
>
>> "Holy, holy, holy,
>> Lord God Almighty,
>> who was and is and is to come!"
>
> Whenever the living creatures give glory and honor and thanks to Him who sits on the throne, who lives forever and ever, the twenty-four elders fall down before Him who sits on the throne and worship Him who lives forever and ever, and cast their crowns before the throne, saying:
>
>> "You are worthy, O Lord,
>> to receive glory and honor and power;
>> for You created all things,
>> and by Your will they exist and were created"
>
> (verses 4-11).

This incredible scene awaits us in heaven, where we will join a great multitude gathered around God's throne. I want to be right in the middle of it all! From Revelation 4:1 on, we do not see any evidence whatsoever of the church anywhere on earth. It is not until Revelation 19:11 that we see the church again in the Scriptures, but this time, she is in heaven, getting ready to return to earth with Jesus Christ, her Lord. What a glorious day that will be!

> Now I saw heaven opened, and behold, a white horse. And He who sat on him was called Faithful and True, and in righteousness He judges and makes war. His eyes were like a flame of fire, and on His head were many crowns. He had a name written that no one knew except Himself. He was clothed with a robe dipped in blood, and His name is called The Word of God. And the armies in heaven, clothed in fine linen, white and clean, followed Him on white horses. Now out of His mouth goes a sharp sword, that with it He should strike the nations. And He Himself will rule them with a rod of iron. He Himself treads the winepress of the fierceness and wrath of Almighty God. And He has on His robe and on His thigh a name written:
>
> KING OF KINGS AND LORD OF LORDS (Revelation 19:11-16).

On that day, we will happily ride atop heaven's steeds. Remember, the only way it would be possible for us to follow Christ from heaven to earth is if we had been raptured upward prior to the tribulation.

Just as you've seen that Scripture makes it clear the church will be raptured, it also differentiates between that event and Christ's second coming—don't confuse the two. I've included a chart here to simplify and explain the differences. And while no means exhaustive, it is a good primer.

The Rapture	Christ's Second Coming
At the rapture, believers will meet the Lord in the air (1 Thessalonians 4:17).	At Christ's second coming, believers will return with Him to the earth (Revelation 19:14-16).
Occurs before the tribulation (Revelation 3:10).	Occurs at the end of the tribulation (Revelation 6-19).

The Rapture	Christ's Second Coming
It is imminent, instant, and exclusive to the church (1 Corinthians 15:50-54).	Takes place after specific end-times events have occurred (2 Thessalonians 2:4), and is visible to all (Revelation 1:7).
Removes believers from the earth as an act of merciful deliverance from God's wrath upon the earth (1 Thessalonians 5:9).	Removes unbelievers in judgment, brings the tribulation to an end, and defeats the Antichrist (Matthew 24:40-41; Revelation 19:19-20).

I cannot stress this enough: No one will want to be an earth-dweller when Jesus Christ returns at His second coming!

The Lord knows who you are and how to deliver you, dear saint. In this age of facial-recognition technology, air travelers can now move through international customs by facing a screen and allowing it to scan their faces, which it does instantly. If a green light appears, the customs door opens. No identification or passport is needed. If we, through technology, can identify others, how much more can God identify us who are marked by His Holy Spirit? We will not be forgotten or left behind when Christ comes for His own! "Watch therefore, and pray always that you may be counted worthy to escape all these things that will come to pass, and to stand before the Son of Man" (Luke 21:36).

THE RAPTURE MOTIVATES

What stimulates, encourages, provokes, and compels you to do what you do? In other words, what motivates you in life? I don't know about you, but when there is a special appointment or a long-awaited event I'm looking forward to, I am motivated to get ready for that day. Christian, you and I have the greatest motivator ever—we have an appointment with the Lord Jesus Christ. How do we get ready for such an important date? "Do this, knowing the time, that now it is high time to awake out of sleep; for now our salvation is nearer than when we first believed. The night is far spent, the day is at hand. Therefore let us cast off the works of darkness, and let us put on the armor of light" (Romans 13:11-12).

These verses assume anticipation because we sense that something is up. The command *do this* makes us realize that the following assignment is not optional. Don't be lulled into a spiritual slumber by scoffers who say, "Where is the promise of His coming? For since the fathers fell asleep, all things continue as they were from the beginning of creation" (2 Peter 3:4). That kind of thinking leads to spiritual stupor.

> Who then is a faithful and wise servant, whom his master made ruler over his household, to give them food in due season? Blessed is that servant whom his master, when he comes, will find so doing. Assuredly, I say to you that he will make him ruler over all his goods. But if that evil servant says in his heart, "My master is delaying his coming," and begins to beat his fellow servants, and to eat and drink with the drunkards… (Matthew 24:45-49).

Did you notice the progression? Did you catch the result of believing the master isn't coming anytime soon?

Jesus said, "Let your waist be girded and your lamps burning; and you yourselves be like men who *wait* for their master" (Luke 12:35-36). Are you waiting for your Master? Jesus is coming back! But it doesn't stop there. Verse 37 says, "Blessed are those servants whom the master, when he comes, will find *watching*." And verse 40, "Therefore you also be ready, for the Son of Man is coming at an hour you do not expect."

Allow me to be brutally honest with some of you. When a doctor says, "You are sick. You've got cancer, and it doesn't look good," he is telling you to set your house in order. And if you hear those words from your doctor, please understand that he is being merciful. He is exhorting you, "Use what time you have left wisely. Ready yourself to meet your Master"—words many Christians need to hear from the Lord today.

Awaken! Wait! Watch! It is incumbent upon every believer to have this mindset. And in doing so, you will be motivated to be "looking for the blessed hope and glorious appearing of our great God and Savior Jesus Christ" (Titus 2:13).

The Christian looking for the blessed hope of Christ's appearing is scanning, searching, and watching the horizon in hope. Does this mean you should quit your job, stop your education, neglect your family, and sit on the rooftop of your house waiting for Jesus? Absolutely not! In a parable, Jesus taught, "Do business till I come" or, as the King James version puts it, "Occupy till I come" (Luke 19:13). Both doing and occupying are a call to action in your sphere of influence. Wherever God has placed you, be a light and witness for Him because time is running out. Every passing moment brings us that much closer to Christ's coming for His church.

Keeping the knowledge that the Lord could come back at any moment in the forefront of our minds encourages us to live differently. "Beloved, now we are children of God; and it has not yet been revealed what we shall be, but we know that when He is revealed, we shall be like Him, for we shall see Him as He is. And everyone who has this hope in Him purifies himself, just as He is pure" (1 John 3:2-3). We cannot imagine how our resurrected bodies will look, but one thing is sure: We will be like Jesus. Wow! We will stand in perfection—free from sin's ramifications—on the day of resurrection. Until then, we must conduct ourselves in purity and righteousness.

Mention the word *righteousness* and immediately some are intimidated, but they shouldn't be. Righteous living means deciding to do the right things—we ponder, pause, hold off speaking or acting, and then choose to do God's will. That is practical day-to-day righteousness. It means we want to do that which glorifies God. We want to invest our time and resources in ways that honor Him.

More than ever, we must be in Christ-honoring fellowship with other believers. Now is not the time to forsake gathering for worship by staying at home and "doing church" online, in the comfort of our living rooms. "Let us think of ways to motivate one another to acts of love and good works. And let us not neglect our meeting together, as some people do, but encourage one another, especially now that the day of His return is drawing near" (Hebrews 10:24-25 NLT).

Wherever God has placed you, be a light and witness for Him because time is running out. Every passing moment brings us that much closer to Christ's coming for His church.

World events are unfolding more quickly than ever, but don't worry. None of them have escaped God's purview. If you are anxiously wondering, *What is God going to do?*, a more important question is, What will you do with what you see and hear? I believe God is asking each of us, "Will you trust Me? Will you put your faith in Me to do what I have promised to do for My people, the church?"

Before I sign my name to an email or a letter, it is always preceded by "Awaiting His Return" because that expresses how I live my life—with joy and excitement, in abandonment to the will of God. I've often been asked, "How are you so confident? Where does your boldness come from?" My answer can be summed up in two short sentences: I know my Redeemer lives. And I know He is coming back for me.

Two thousand years have passed since Titus 2:13 was written—meaning every generation of believers is to live with expectant hope of the rapture. The possibility of the rapture happening at any time should fill your heart to overflowing at the thought of the goodness and mercy of God. My friend, how are you living? Are you eagerly looking for the "blessed hope and glorious appearing of our great God and Savior Jesus Christ"?

I pray you are. It could be today!

CHAPTER 12

TODAY IS THE BEST DAY

✝

Spoken or written, for better or worse, the last words of any individual can be some of the most memorable. Can you remember the angry words a friend said before they walked away, never to be seen again? Or the gems whispered by a loved one as they passed from this life to the next? Last words matter.

I have a habit that may sound strange to some, but it works for me. I frequently read the last chapter of a book first. "Why?" you ask. It's simple. I understand a book better when I read the end first. And sometimes, an author's last words carry the biggest punch—the climax, the grand reveal that answers the mystery, or the one sentence that explains everything perfectly. Those last words often contain the author's most tender, significant, or meaningful thoughts, which is true of the apostle Peter's final epistle. Peter gained a tremendous amount of wisdom over his decades of ministry. That is why it is essential for us to consider some of Peter's last words concerning the attitudes, doctrines, and dangers we should hold to or watch out for in these last days.

IT'S A GOOD DAY TO BE ALIVE

Why is it that after thousands of years, people around the globe still gather to study the Bible? It is because they are convinced beyond a shadow of a doubt that the Word of God anticipated this moment. More than one-quarter of the Bible deals with eschatology—the study of prophecy and the last days. The advent of God's promised Messiah is identified with the "last days" (Hebrews 1:2), and I want to point out that Jesus' birth fulfilled Isaiah 7:14, Isaiah 9:6, and Micah 5:2. Why is this important? Because you cannot know for certain if the New Testament is true without its Old Testament background. It's impossible.

If you read only the New Testament, you could easily think it's a collection of stories. And if you don't know the Old, you will never understand that what transpired in the New Testament era fulfilled what the prophets spoke of. Churches that skip the study of God's prophetic teachings do so to their detriment. The challenge upon us is recognizing what the whole of Scripture says concerning our day and age.

Theologically, the birth of Jesus Christ began the ticking of the prophetic time clock of the last days. And if we looked at the passage of time and fulfilled prophecies in a linear sense, the lateness of our current hour would be shockingly apparent. The events making headlines today are those that the prophets wrote of. And if men like Martin Luther, John Wesley, or Charles Spurgeon could see what we are witnessing, their jaws would drop. One day, a man approached me and said, "I've read about this time all my life, and now it's here. I knew it would come because the Bible said it would. I just didn't envision it would happen like it is."

In a 2002 *60 Minutes* interview with Morley Safer, the late comedian Robin Williams joked, "I only ever play Vegas one night at a time. It's a hideous, gaudy place; it may not be the end of the world per se, but you can certainly see it from there." We chuckle at Williams's vision of the end of the world, but our preoccupation with it is longstanding. The Pennsylvania Academy of the Fine Arts houses an 1817 oil painting by Benjamin West titled *Death on the Pale Horse*. West rendered his version of the end based on Revelation 6:8, in which the rider of the pale horse of the Apocalypse ravages the earth.

In more recent history, we've lived through a global pandemic and are continually warned of catastrophes looming on the horizon. People viewed the COVID-19 virus as ushering in the end of the world. It didn't, but I urge you to be careful about which end you are focusing on—the end of the world as we know it or the end of the church on earth. They are two very different events. The first event ends in catastrophe and causes a fatalistic outlook. The second is thrilling, ushers in pure bliss, and fosters thanksgiving, hope, and joy.

The condition of the world you and I live in makes it clear that no one, not our leaders nor the general public, knows what comes next. Only the God of the Bible knows the future, and before it comes to pass, He declared it (Isaiah 42:9). We know from Scripture that difficulties do lay ahead, yet God's prophetic Word serves as an encouragement for us to trust and believe that whatever happens does so under His watchful eye and sovereign control.

It's tempting to look around, reckon all hope lost, and say, "Stop the world! I want to get off!" People say things like that because they want to escape the craziness or confusion of life. And we understand why nonbelievers would have that attitude—they're terrified. But the Christian who knows and understands the Bible will say with excitement, "Wow. I can't believe this is happening right in front of me. Thank You, Lord, for allowing me to be alive right now, and to have this front-row seat to the future!"

IT'S A GOOD DAY TO KNOW YOU ARE LOVED

I'm not sure what your perception of God's grace is, but I want you to know that it is beyond powerful. As difficulties intensify in these unprecedented times, you have no reason to fear the future. God's grace will be upped, turbocharged, and tailor made for you, His beloved.

Peter addressed his last words to a special group of people he called "beloved" (2 Peter 3:1). This tender word singled them out as worthy ones, favored ones, who are of grace. Oh, how we need to hear this in today's crazy, out-of-control, mixed-up world! As God's beloved, His heart is for you, His eyes are upon you, and He has targeted you as a recipient of His divine grace. Jesus went so far as to call you friend (John 15:15). You can have 1,000-plus friends on social media who will like you one minute and unfriend you the next, but there is only one friend who truly counts—Jesus.

The world won't love you and doesn't necessarily want to be your friend, which is why being beloved is so precious. God loves you. Let those three simple words soak in. Let them saturate your soul. "Behold what manner of love the Father has bestowed on us, that we should be called children of God!" (1 John 3:1). Have you sat at the Father's table for a while and those words lost a bit of their impact? I hope not! Because for someone who has never heard that the Creator God of the universe loves them, and wants them in His family, those words are astounding.

> God loves you. Let those three simple words soak in. Let them saturate your soul.

The next time you hold your Bible, I want you to find the first three chapters of Genesis and hold them between your forefinger and thumb. Those pages detail the creation of the universe and all living things, Adam and Eve in the garden of Eden, the serpent's temptation, and the fall of Adam and Eve. What's left? The rest of the entire Bible—the part where God says, "I love you. You've been wayward and estranged from Me; please come back. This is what I will do to save you and give your life purpose." That, my friend, is how much you are loved!

IT'S A GOOD DAY TO BE REMINDED

The Bible encourages us to have the mind of God (1 Corinthians 2:16). That doesn't mean you can be as smart or wise as God or know what He knows. To have the mind of God is to have your mind continually renewed in the Scriptures. Peter understands this and says, "I now write to you...[to] stir up your pure minds by way of reminder" (2 Peter 3:1). What Peter is saying is, "I want to arouse you completely regarding spiritual things. I want you to be fully awake or stimulated." It's like he wants to take us by the shoulders, shake us, and say, "Listen to me!" To "stir up" is to bring to the top what is at the bottom. What does that mean? It means that A: I am going to recall something from memory. Or B: I want you to give me prompts to help me remember what I already know. Peter is writing to his fellow beloved ones because he wants them to recall or recollect God's plan for their lives. But in the original Greek language, the meaning goes even further.

Our English words *stir up* are one word in the Greek language, *anazao*. And when you read the definition, you are going to think of the modern usage of the word *woke*. Yes, you read correctly. *Stir up* means to be woke, to spring up, to be completely awake, fully alert and aware of what is going on. It also means to rub in, to score, or etch something, like kids carving their initials on a tree so their handiwork is permanent. The Bible is telling us we need to etch God's Word into our minds and hearts.

Repetition is one of the strongest teachers available to us, but as a rule, we don't like it because we think it's boring. If you are a sloppy or indifferent student, that attitude will significantly hinder your learning capabilities because you'll hear repetitive instruction and think, *I've heard this before. I know it.* But let me ask: Do you really know what you're hearing as well as you think you do? Peter was not concerned with how well his readers could repeat his words. He wanted them to *know* God's words deep down inside, in a way that affected their lives.

I am a by-product of a man I've already mentioned, Pastor Chuck Smith. Pastor Chuck would deliver a sermon, walk into his office, and throw his notes in the trash because he never wanted to use them again. He wanted fresh material, fresh insight from the Holy Spirit, the next time he taught that text. My wife worked in Chuck's office, and she would grab his discarded notes and give them to me. I still have a stack of them—you would be shocked by how simple they are. Pastor Chuck would write points A, B, and C, along with maybe a verse or two, then expound on what was deep within him for an hour. He was saturated with the Word of God, and his messages came out of a well of recollection. That type of knowledge should be every believer's desire.

One of the many traits that made Pastor Chuck's teaching remarkable was the way he used repetition. He would read a chapter or passage, set his Bible down, and quote it again verbatim while never looking down. He would repeat it roughly three more times during the message—repeat, repeat, repeat. Lazy listeners were probably irritated and bored at hearing the same words over and over. But those eager to learn didn't mind because the Holy Spirit was etching lasting spiritual truths into their hearts and minds—and they got it! I thank God for allowing me to be one of the many thousands who sat under his expositional teachings.

Likewise, politicians understand the power of repetition and have perfected it to their advantage. How do I know? Choose any politician and watch their rallies. On Monday, they'll give a speech. Then they'll hop on a plane and give the same speech on Tuesday and Thursday in other locations. Why? In their desire to influence you, they know that reiterating a certain policy or promise again and again and again will pay off come election day.

Politics aside, repetition is an effective means of communicating what you want others to retain, and we see that in God's Word—specifically, the four Gospels. Why are there four? To etch into your mind a complete 360-degree picture of Jesus Christ's life and deeds from four different angles.

Regular reminders from the Word are also a strong defense against destructive heresy. Like Peter, Paul repeated himself when writing to believers. "My brethren, rejoice in the Lord. For me to write the same things to you is not tedious, but for you it is safe" (Philippians 3:1). Without the whole counsel of God stored deep within you, false teachers and their teachings sound plausible. That is why we must continually remind ourselves of the gospel that brings us into a right relationship with God.

In our stress-filled, preoccupied lives, we tend to forget what is important, making reminders essential. Here are a few that I trust will act as a fortress to your soul.

> I know the thoughts that I think toward you, says the LORD, thoughts of peace and not of evil, to give you a future and a hope (Jeremiah 29:11).

True or false? True!

> How precious also are Your thoughts to me, O God!
> How great is the sum of them!
> If I should count them, they would be more in number than the sand;
> when I awake, I am still with You (Psalm 139:17-18).

True or false? True!

> If anyone is in Christ, he is a new creation; old things have passed away; behold, all things have become new (2 Corinthians 5:17).

True or false? True!

> The Lord has appeared of old to me, saying:
> "Yes, I have loved you with an everlasting love; therefore with lovingkindness I have drawn you" (Jeremiah 31:3).

True or false? True!

> Come to Me, all you who labor and are heavy laden, and I will give you rest. Take My yoke upon you and learn from Me, for I am gentle and lowly in heart, and you will find rest for your souls. For My yoke is easy and My burden is light (Matthew 11:28-30).

True or false? True! In fact, it is so true that when Christ enters someone's life, He alleviates the weight of their burdens by lifting them onto His shoulders. You may not see it on their face or posture, but the reality is there, nonetheless. And it is freeing!

These five passages can change the course of our lives. Rehearse them and repeat them liberally.

IT'S A GOOD DAY TO KNOW THE WITNESS OF GOD

When called upon, witnesses are to testify of what they know is true. According to 2 Peter 3:2, "the words which were spoken before by the holy prophets, and the commandment of us, the apostles of the Lord and Savior," were faithful witnesses. The inclusion of the phrase "the commandment of us" may make it sound like Peter and the other apostles made up a new rule. Not so. The "commandment of us" was a repetition of and in obedience to the previous written testimony of the prophets.

It is important to note that the New Testament authors began writing approximately 50 years after the death of Christ. The only Scripture available to early believers was the Old Testament, and they used it to verify that what they saw and were being taught was true (Acts 17:11).

One of the most powerful sermons ever preached—and a perfect example of repeating the witness of God—was given by Stephen and recorded by Luke in Acts 7. Stephen was one of Jesus' followers, a student of the apostles, full of faith and of the Holy Spirit (Acts 6:5). The account of Stephen is extraordinary for a couple of reasons.

First, Stephen was one of seven disciples chosen to give widows their daily distribution of food so that the apostles could focus on teaching. He served the widows faithfully, but Scripture also says he "did great wonders and signs among the people" (Acts 6:8). His wisdom and witness could not be disputed or resisted. Stephen's bold faith infuriated some to the point of calling false witnesses to accuse him of blasphemy and have him arrested (Acts 6:10-13).

What will you do if you are falsely accused and arrested for your faith? Given the current culture of intolerance, it could happen. If I am ever put in that position, I want to do exactly as Stephen did. He gave his captors a fantastic Bible study straight out of the Old Testament! I encourage you to read it in its entirety in Acts 7.

The scope of Stephen's sermon is the second point I want you to consider. Outside of Jesus' Sermon on the Mount, it is the longest sermon in the New Testament. Stephen covered Israel's history from Abraham to Christ. He knew it well and used it to clearly show that Jesus was the Messiah promised by the prophets.

Logical people would have been swayed by the irrefutable evidence of their own scriptures, but Luke records that though Stephen's listeners were "cut to the heart," "they gnashed at him with their teeth" (Acts 7:54). Can you imagine the degree of anger that provokes someone to grind their teeth at another person? They hated him. They hated his words enough to stone him. "But he, being full of the Holy Spirit, gazed into heaven and saw the glory of God, and Jesus standing at the right hand of God, and said, 'Look! I see the heavens opened and the Son of Man standing at the right hand of God!'" (verses 55-56).

Stephen was dying—martyred for speaking the truth—and Jesus, the Alpha and Omega, the Beginning and the End, the Almighty stood to receive him. Yet Scripture says Jesus is currently seated at the Father's right hand (see Ephesians 1:20; Hebrews 8:1). Is there a contradiction? No. And I believe this has a biblical foundation. Because Scripture tells us that Jesus "comes" for His church at the rapture, why would He not stand to receive His beloved child at this critical moment?

When you are fully persuaded that Jesus Christ—the Messiah foretold by the prophets—commands your destiny, you will be unwavering in the face of opposition. You will stand bold in your faith.

Last words or not, it is impossible to fully gauge the impact of what we say on this side of heaven. But because we're looking at last words, let's add Stephen's: "Lord, do not charge them with this sin" (Acts 7:60). That is one powerful prayer when you consider that standing among the crowd was Saul of Tarsus (Acts 8:1). Saul, the zealous persecutor and enemy of Christians, whom you know as the apostle Paul.

IT'S A GOOD DAY TO GET READY

At one time or another, you've probably demanded, "Are you ready?" of a dawdling child, sluggish teen, never-on-time friend, late wife, or distracted husband. But let me ask it another way: "Are you ready *today?*" Are you ready right now to take on whatever or whoever comes your way spiritually?

What, or rather, who, should we be ready for? Peter said it's scoffers who mock, belittle, or outright deny two fundamental doctrines: the coming of Jesus Christ and God's creation of the heavens and earth. Do you know anyone who makes light of your expectation that Jesus will return or pokes fun at your belief that God created all things? How important are these issues to you? The truths about Christ's return and the beginning of creation should be of supreme importance because according to Peter, in the last days, scoffers will target those issues.

Second Peter 3:4 tells us what these scoffers will say: "Where is the promise of His coming? For since the fathers fell asleep, all things continue as they were from the beginning of creation." You can almost hear someone mocking, "Jesus promised to return. Are you joking? That is ridiculous!" The tone of verse 4 implies that God doesn't know or doesn't care, and it's questionable whether God even exists.

But the Bible assumes a fact a scoffer does not. "The fool has said in his heart, 'There is no God'" (Psalm 14:1). Notice the Bible doesn't say, "The fool has said in his mind, 'There is no God.'" The reason a fool doesn't say that is because his mind is in conflict with his heart. The word "said" means to repeat it over and over. What is the fool attempting to do? Overrule their mind with one emotionally driven excuse piled atop another. But their mind knows better.

Second Peter 3:16 defines scoffers and mockers as untaught, unstable people who twist the Scriptures. It isn't that they cannot learn. Mockers refuse to learn because they've already made up their mind to bend the Bible to fit their desires. Is it possible for someone to willfully forget to their detriment? Romans 1:28 says yes. "Even as they did not like to retain God in their knowledge, God gave them over to a debased mind."

It's a given that nonbelievers will ridicule your beliefs, but scoffers are not exclusive to secular settings. Liberal pulpiteers are shamelessly espousing doctrinal lies, seeking to nullify the power of the church in the world.

Scoffers make unfounded statements saying there is no indication that Jesus Christ is coming back, which proves they're "walking according to their own lusts" (2 Peter 3:3). When we think of lust, we assume it refers to a pornographic mindset, but that isn't all it means. It also means the desire to promote man above God. Unbelievers conclude that if the earth is still evolving and humanity is progressively getting better, there is no need for Jesus to return. And in fact, for that to happen would be inconvenient.

A scoffer's carnal state renders them unwilling or unable to spiritually discern the signs of the times much like the religious leaders of Jesus' day. The Pharisees and Sadducees banded together and asked Jesus to show them a "sign from heaven" (Matthew 16:1). Jesus answered, "When it is evening you say, 'It will be fair weather, for the sky is red'" (verse 2). Maybe you've heard the saying, "Red sky at night, sailor's delight." The reason a red sky at night is a "sailor's delight" is because it means the storm has passed, the clouds have broken up, and the red sky is an indicator of that.

Jesus continued: "And in the morning, 'It will be foul weather today, for the sky is red and threatening.' Hypocrites! You know how to discern the face of the sky, but you cannot discern the signs of the times. A wicked and adulterous generation seeks after a sign, and no sign shall be given to it except the sign of the prophet Jonah. And He left them and departed" (verses 3-4). The ability to forecast the weather wasn't Jesus' concern. These outwardly religious men were flirting with every kind of spirituality except the truth, and for that, Jesus called them a wicked and adulterous generation and walked away without another word.

If they had any hair on their neck, it would have stood up because they understood what Jesus was saying. Jonah was in the belly of a great fish three days and three nights (see Jonah 1:17), and when released, Jonah came forth as a prophet of doom to the city of Nineveh. His assignment was to tell the people the truth concerning their future. Unless they repented, God had condemned them to destruction. Judgment—that was the sign Jesus would give to the Pharisees and Sadducees. And today, we are to warn this age of God's coming judgment.

The Pharisees and Sadducees asked for proof, a sign, that Jesus was the Messiah. What about you? Are you looking for a sign? I cannot assume that you are a Christ-follower simply because you are reading this. Notice that I didn't say Christian. In this day and age, people are quick to say, "I'm a Christian," yet believe something entirely at odds with the Bible. Do you need to see a sign before you'll believe? If so, beware. If seeing a sign is what it will take to make you believe, then the implication is that not seeing a sign can result in unbelief.

The fact that Jesus told the highly educated and prominent religious scoffers of His day that a wicked and adulterous generation seeks after a sign should act as a warning. Despite abundant evidence, those who keep sarcastically taunting, "Prove it to me" will eventually embrace falsehoods. We cannot afford to close our eyes to their presence within the church. When it comes to confronting scoffers, nowhere does the Bible say to be polite or tolerant. We must be ready to refute and rebuke.

IT'S A GOOD DAY TO GET WISE

Good science and the Bible always align with one another, yet some of the same people mocking Christ's return also deny the creative power of God in forming the universe. That type of nonsensical and irrational teaching goes against what the entire Bible announces while ignoring the intricacies of the heavens and earth that demand a Designer. You don't hear pure Darwinism touted within scientific circles like you used to, and that is because it's a bit of an embarrassment.

Discoveries in archaeology, anthropology, and biochemistry have upended Charles Darwin's theory of random mutation/natural selection. "If you search the scientific literature on evolution, and if you focus your search on the question of how molecular machines—the basis of life—developed, you will find an eerie and complete silence,"[1] said American biochemist Michael Behe.

Even though God provides ample evidence of His existence through nature, scoffers work hard at pushing this out of their minds. Here is where it begins:

> They willfully forget: that by the word of God the heavens were of old, and the earth standing out of water and in the water (2 Peter 3:5).
>
> In the beginning God created the heavens and the earth. The earth was without form, and void; and darkness was on the face of the deep. And the Spirit of God was hovering over the face of the waters (Genesis 1:1-2).
>
> Then God said, "Let there be a firmament in the midst of the waters, and let it divide the waters from the waters." Thus God made the firmament, and divided the waters which were under the firmament from the waters which were above the firmament; and it was so (Genesis 1:6-7).

This is amazing! Genesis says that at creation, the earth was in water before it stood out of water. Earth was a watery sphere until God's Word went forth and the Spirit of God moved over the face of the deep. The King James version uses the word "hovering" in Genesis 1:2, but it can also be translated as *brooded*, which means to stir up. The waters began to separate so that there were waters below and waters above. That is a radical scientific truth!

We live at the bottom of an invisible ocean called the atmosphere, a layer of gases surrounding our planet.[2] And yet, the earth is, in a sense, coming out of the water because two-thirds of our planet is covered in water.

How was it possible for Peter, a first-century fisherman, to make a 100-percent true scientific statement that would remain undiscovered for millennia? He knew the Genesis account of creation as recorded in the Bible. God's Word preceded mankind's discovery of well-known scientific truths. Here are a few that relate to the earth.

The earth has a rain cycle.

> He draws up drops of water,
> which distill as rain from the mist (Job 36:27).

The earth is round, not flat.

> It is He who sits above the circle of the earth,
> and its inhabitants are like grasshoppers,
> who stretches out the heavens like a curtain,
> and spreads them out like a tent to dwell in
> (Isaiah 40:22).

The earth floats in space.

> He stretches out the north over empty space;
> He hangs the earth on nothing (Job 26:7).

There are paths or currents in the sea.

> The birds of the air,
> and the fish of the sea
> that pass through the paths of the seas (Psalm 8:8).

Scientists have proven the above Bible verses to be factual millennia after they were written. Scholars estimate that Job lived 3,500 to 4,000 years ago! When it comes to trusting the whole of Scripture, let me put the importance of the creation account this way: If you accept Genesis 1:1, "In the beginning, God created the heavens and the earth," the rest is details. In other words, the biblical account of creation is a fundamental doctrine. It is not open to debate or the scoffer's dangerous revisions undermining the trustworthiness of what follows.

The same Bible that says God created the fantastic sphere that you and I call home also declares Jesus will return. I relish the thought!

Do you belong to the family of God? Are you hanging on to His Word and growing in it? Great! Are you vigilant concerning spiritual things? Stay the course and live out your faith enthusiastically, because today is a good day to be alive! Christ could come any time.

CHAPTER 13

HEADING FOR HOME

What do you think of when you hear the announcement, "I'm heading for home"? If you're a coach watching your runner round third base, there is a bit of nervous excitement. But if your boss says those same words at the end of a hectic 12-hour day, there's probably a sigh of relief. And how about the last day of vacation? Everybody knows it was a vacation away when they've had enough and want to go home. Thankfully, no matter how often we go home in this world, believers are not truly home yet. According to the Bible, God's people are pilgrims in a foreign land, and our hearts beat with longing for our real home, heaven.

You've read bits and pieces about heaven throughout this book, and for good reason—God wants you to be excited about heaven. If you know the love, grace, and mercy of God in Jesus Christ, His Son, you should be shouting, "Let's go!" Are your thoughts of heaven exhilarating? I pray so. Because when they are, your life will transcend today's headlines, deadlines, worries, or cares.

It's true we live, work, and play here. But more importantly, we want to be used by God to speak truth and live a life activated by the things of God, and yet we can't wait to reach our heavenly destination.

Why is that true? Because Ecclesiastes 3:11 tells us, "He has made everything beautiful in its time. Also He has put eternity in their hearts." There is a natural curiosity within humans that causes us to think about life after death—to wonder what comes next. For the believer, that curiosity gives way to a sense of longing because faith looks forward, always forward. Faith thinks about eternity.

HEAVEN IS WAITING

What if you came home after a long and challenging journey only to find your front door flung wide open ready and waiting for you to enter? You'd drop your bags and rush in. Every believer will experience, at the very least, that same level of excitement and more because the Bible promises, "An entrance will be supplied to you abundantly into the everlasting kingdom of our Lord and Savior Jesus Christ" (2 Peter 1:11).

Few homes today have grand entrances, so to better understand what is implied in the word "entrance," we must step back in time. The term suggests a realm or kingdom where wars and rumors of wars are talked of, and the possibility of a siege is real, like those in the Middle Ages.

Many medieval castles had an enormous entrance gate in the outer wall that, when lowered, extended over a moat. In the middle of that big gate was a little door. The little door was well-lit, and couriers could go through it, but the gate was never let down unless soldiers were going out to war or returning from it.

Sentries were positioned atop the castle walls, ready with crossbows as they scanned the landscape. If a lone figure appeared off in the distance, the sentries would shout to one another, "Somebody's coming! Be alert. Watch!" As the silhouette drew closer, they would look to see if he wore the colors of their kingdom and his banner bore the king's insignia. And if so, the watchmen shouted, "Open the gate!" Immediately, that messenger warrior would hear sounds of metal clanging and gears grinding as the massive gate was lowered. His grand reception by citizens, dignitaries, and the King himself, would let him know he was indeed home.

I've described a word picture here, but one day, you won't need help picturing what it's like to enter heaven's gates!

Some people assume that the popular images of heaven featuring chubby, baby-faced angels plucking harps are an accurate portrayal of heaven. Or they've visualized heaven as a bright, monochromatic, sterile place. But who wants either of those scenarios for all eternity? I don't, and the Bible doesn't describe heaven in those ways.

At first sight, visitors to the Yosemite Valley's stunning granite monoliths are often left awestruck. If that is the response to the grandeur and beauty of a fallen world, we can only imagine what we will experience in heaven. I believe we will be utterly speechless upon our entrance to heaven. We'll see fantastic angelic creatures who are truly beyond words. The music will be as we've never heard sung or played before—beautiful beyond belief, powerful, majestic—and when all the saints join in, loud! There will be trees and rivers and animals. I encourage you to read the book *Heaven* by Randy Alcorn. His theological work on the doctrine of heaven will enlarge your thinking. And while the Bible doesn't give us every detail about heaven, one thing is certain: It will be glorious!

Have you noticed how conversations centered on heaven produce a sweet camaraderie among believers? Something deep within us thrills at the prospect of reuniting with family and friends who have already arrived. "Every joy on earth—including the joy of reunion—is an inkling, a whisper of greater joy."[1] And then there is the anticipation of meeting the heroic Christians we've only heard and read about.

Personally, I want to meet Noah, and I can't wait to sit down with Israeli commando General Joshua. I want to tell him that I read his book often, and it has inspired me to be courageous and take a bold stand. I am sure that we'll trade accounts of battles won and lost and glorify God for what He did in and through our lives. And then I hope we'll go off to visit Deborah—she was amazing.

God called Deborah to a prominent position as a prophetess and Israel's judge when bold male leadership was scarce (see Judges 4–5). Deborah was going about her daily business until she heard that Israel was being threatened. She called for one of the military commanders, Barak, to tell him that the Lord had commanded him to lead Israel's troops into battle. Barak's lackluster response probably surprised her: "If you will go with me, then I will go; but if you will not go with me, I will not go!" (Judges 4:8). Deborah agreed, confident that God would bring them success, and He did. Read further, and you learn that it was an unassuming yet fearless woman, Jael, who struck the final blow against the enemy's commander to help secure Israel's victory.

The account of Deborah, Barak, and Jael reminds us that whether male or female, we are called to seize every opportunity God puts before us.

A day is coming when we will have breathed our last or we will hear the rapture's trumpet blast, and it will be clear—we are going home. An entrance will be opened wide for believers because they are at peace with God. Jesus broke death and the fear of it so that we can say with King David, "Yea, though I walk through the valley of the shadow of death, I will fear no evil" (Psalm 23:4). All our suffering on this side of eternity is merely a shadow of death.

However heaven comes to you or me, it could very well arrive sooner than anticipated, and that reality is the propellant, the accelerant, that drives the believer—is it not? Faced with a world in opposition to biblical truth, we realize the battle is now. We have but a brief opportunity to be the people of God here on earth. One day, there will be no gauntlet to run, no test of faith. Today is the test of faith! It is here. Now is the time to be a Deborah or Jael. Now is the time to be a Joshua.

HEAVEN'S HOPE

Is your heartbeat in sync with the heartbeat of the God of heaven? Because if it is, it will motivate your life. The heartbeat of heaven within us is proof of God's presence in our life. Thankfully, God hasn't relegated Himself to a temple made of stone. That would be equal to the Lion of the tribe of Judah living in a zoo. He lives within us, and when our hearts beat with heaven's, it generates hope. Romans 8:24-25 says, "We were saved in this hope, but hope that is seen is not hope; for why does one still hope for what he sees? But if we hope for what we do not see, we eagerly wait for it with perseverance."

You do not hope for that which you already possess. You've got it. It's yours. A teenager might dream of owning a car, eagerly hoping that dream becomes a reality, and the sooner, the better. But once they have a vehicle, that long-awaited hope is satisfied. Believer, our hope goes way beyond any earthly desire. And its arrival is guaranteed.

Grammatically speaking, the words "were saved" in Romans 8:24 is a compound past-tense phrase in the original New Testament Greek. This is exciting! Why? Let's allow the Bible to answer that question: "Blessed be the God and Father of our Lord Jesus Christ, who has blessed us with every spiritual blessing in the heavenly places in Christ, just as He chose us in Him before the foundation of the world" (Ephesians 1:3-4). The apostle Paul speaks from God's perspective—He looks at you and sees Jesus—and every bit of what has transpired as a result of your salvation is described in the past tense. Simply stated, your eternal home has been secured for you because of the blood of Christ. Think of the ramifications for your life!

Because of Jesus Christ, heaven is guaranteed, so why allow fears of what might happen tomorrow to trip you up? Your arrival in heaven is not only your hope, it also provides the basis for a glorious freedom in Christ—a beautiful boldness—now. Once the heartbeat of heaven begins stirring in your heart, I guarantee your perspective will change because the expectation of heaven is transformative.

But maybe you're feeling a little down, your thoughts are wandering, worries have crept in, and you feel off. I love how the late Dr. Charles Stanley said to remedy the situation.

Years ago, I watched Dr. Stanley teach on Ephesians 1:3, and he said this verse demands that you "preach it to yourself." Then he pulled open the collar of his shirt, looked down at himself, and asked, "Why are you cast down, O my soul? And why are you disquieted within me? Hope in God, for I shall yet praise Him for the help of His countenance" (Psalm 42:5). I cannot articulate all that it means to have God, in a moment that you least expect, smile or put His countenance upon your life. In a feeble attempt, let me say it's like having someone walk through a door, light up the room of your soul, and give you a thumbs up before walking away. Experiencing the smile of God here and now creates an eager expectation for all that we'll experience in eternity. We can't see it, but we eagerly wait for it.

HEAVEN'S HELP

The hope of heaven assures us of the help of heaven. The psalmist said, "My help comes from the LORD, who made heaven and earth" (Psalm 121:2). If God made heaven and earth, can He not help you now? Will He not provide for you better than He does for the birds of the air and lilies of the field? (Matthew 6:25-33). The answer is yes, because God is listening. "The Spirit also helps in our weaknesses. For we do not know what we should pray for as we ought, but the Spirit Himself makes intercession for us with groanings which cannot be uttered" (Romans 8:26).

The Greek word *proseuchomai* means "to pray" or "to make a prayer" and emphasizes personal and often heartfelt communication with God. When viewed in that way, prayer becomes a form of worship or *proskuneo* in the Greek language. To *proskuneo* is to worship, bow down, or kiss the hand. Believers are called into a close and loving relationship with God, and *proskuneo* opens our understanding as the connection between prayer and intimacy with our Lord. Intimate times of prayer are opportunities to bring our needs to our heavenly Father, yet how often do we think of God, hand cupped to ear, as it were, waiting to hear from us?

You and I are the same in this way—our origin is one of weakness in the sense that we are born with humanity's general weaknesses: frailty, disease, distress, mental and physical ailments. We all will agree this world hurts! But make no mistake, heaven is listening. The question is, how often are we sending our requests heavenward? How often are we, through tears and cries for help, asking the Lord to instruct and lead and guide us? Not often enough, despite the Bible's assurance that the Holy Spirit will come to our aid. He is standing ready to help us in our weakest moments.

When Scripture says that the "Holy Spirit helps," it means to take hold of. It implies that the Spirit of God takes hold of one end of a heavy log. You might be thinking, *Well, that's great for His end, but what about my end?* You may not like my answer, but this is where you are called to daily pick up your cross and follow Jesus. In the issues of life, the Holy Spirit will help carry your load, but you must obediently go with Him.

I know life can feel overwhelming at times. But let me ask you: When Jesus commanded His disciples to get into a boat and cross over the sea, did He know the wind and waves would be contrary? He did. And He sent them out anyway, knowing full well that He would meet them amidst the storm. Jesus even commanded Peter to leave the safety of the boat and come to Him—wind, water, waves, and all. "When he [Peter] saw that the wind was boisterous, he was afraid; and beginning to sink he cried out, saying, 'Lord, save me!' And immediately Jesus stretched out His hand and caught him" (Matthew 14:30-31).

Three short words—Peter's cry is the shortest recorded prayer in the New Testament. The length or eloquence of your prayer is inconsequential to God. Long or short, wordy or not, heaven is listening and will act in your time of need.

HEAVEN'S CONFIDENCE

To put faith in action requires commitment and diligence. You must stay focused. "Brethren, be even more diligent to make your call and election sure, for if you do these things you will never stumble" (2 Peter 1:10). Whose call is Peter referring to? This is not a generic call. It is yours and only yours—not your best friend's or your grandmother's. How does this relate to the doctrine of election? Both calling and election involve God's divine foreknowledge.

Regarding the doctrine of foreknowledge, the Bible tells us from cover to cover that calling, election, and predestination are based on God's foreknowledge. Therefore, never start a conversation regarding election without beginning with foreknowledge. The believer's calling and election doesn't come about by divine fiat whereby God says, "This section goes to heaven, and that group over there goes to hell." Election doesn't work that way because of His foreknowledge.

God knew from eternity past (foreknowledge) those who would be His and those who would reject Him. God did not suddenly learn that you were His on the day you heard the gospel presentation and accepted His offer of salvation. God knew that you were His child before Jupiter was flung into space. Who gets the credit for you being in heaven? God does. He provided the way of salvation. What about your aunt who winds up in hell? Is God responsible? No. She also heard the message of salvation, perhaps many times, and yet said, "I don't want anything to do with Jesus." She, like so many others, refused the free gift of salvation even though the Spirit pleaded with her, "Take it! Take it!" Eventually, the time for acceptance expired.

By default, all who reject Christ are whisked away to hell because that is where they choose to go.

When you consider that in eternity past God knew you would be with Him forever, is it possible to be or feel more secure? Yes, it is. To prove my point, read Romans 8:28-30 slowly, carefully, and savor every word.

> We know that all things work together for good to those who love God, to those who are the called according to His purpose. For whom He foreknew, He also predestined to be conformed to the image of His Son, that He might be the firstborn among many brethren. Moreover whom He predestined, these He also called; whom He called, these He also justified; and whom He justified, these He also glorified.

The Christian's confidence shouldn't be proud. There is no arrogance or self-righteousness connected to the certainty of our salvation. It is simply a foundational fact of salvation that requires you to "work out your own salvation with fear and trembling" (Philippians 2:12). You have already obtained salvation. Now, you must pick up your feet and move on from "the elementary principles of Christ" (Hebrews 6:1) *because* you are secure. That is faith in action. Someone once said regarding this verse, "Brothers and sisters, work hard." I like that.

Believer, judge yourself daily according to the Scriptures. Confirm that you are indeed among God's children while simultaneously allowing God to put you in places to be used for His glory because "it is God who works in you" (Philippians 2:13). You don't do the work. God works it out in you and through you. And it is His pleasure to do so.

I believe the outworking of the hope of heaven creates assurance, which, in turn, fosters a powerful conviction that God has a specific purpose for my life and yours. Yet I have also seen the opposite at work in Christians who are insecure in their salvation. Christianity is meant to be actively lived out, yet some equate faith to a shiny new car. They lack the confidence to take their faith out of the garage and drive it around town. "It could get bumped or scratched." Good! "But I'll need to change the oil and rotate the tires." True. Regular maintenance keeps faith ready on demand. So, drive it, drive it, drive it!

Parking our faith guarantees it goes nowhere, and because it's going nowhere, we don't see God moving. And when we don't see God moving, we end up with a lack of confidence because we aren't witnessing God's power in action.

When put to the test, faith confirms that it is strong, durable, resilient—able to handle whatever comes its way. It's built to last.

HEAVEN'S OUTWORKING

The necessity of renewed devotion and revival invariably comes up in Sunday sermons and at Christian conferences. I believe that we need to stop talking about making revival happen and start acting like it's already a reality.

You may be thinking, *Okay, but aren't we supposed to pray for the Holy Spirit to move? Pray for people to get saved?* Yes, on both counts. But hear me out.

Does God want to move in your specific church, as well as in your life? He does. So, act like it. Does He want to reach and save the lost? Absolutely! Don't wait to actively reach out to them. We shouldn't be talking about revival as a future event. We should be acting like revived people now. And when we do, God will pour out His Spirit. How can we be so confident? It's all rolled up in the word *do* in 2 Peter 1:10: "If you do these things you will never stumble."

When we determine to do what God has called us to, He has already supplied everything needed to do so. God has paid our way with His Son's blood, moved the pieces of our lives into place, and given us what to say to the audience He supplies. What is our role? Obey! In eternity past, God provided what you need for an effective faith that takes you to heaven, but you must keep on keeping on. Allow me to illustrate.

Scripture calls you and me the bride of Christ, and when it comes to "staying at it" in our Christian faith, it's much like what happens in a marriage.

Marriage is terrific, but as the months and years go by, you discover that you and your spouse are not always on the same wavelength. This could involve anything from who does certain household chores to the expression of intimacy—the issue is unimportant, the outcome greatly so. If you are waiting for the sun, moon, and stars to align before you act, you might be waiting a very long time. Likewise, as believers, we've committed ourselves to Christ—as a bride to her groom—yet we won't always feel motivated to do what He asks. What do you do when that happens? The same things you do when you are devoted to your spouse—don't give up, do the right thing, and keep at it until your heart kicks in.

Perhaps you're feeling unmotivated in the spiritual realm because your faith has weakened or become bruised and battered. The Holy Spirit anticipated this would happen. Isaiah 42:3 says, "A bruised reed He will not break, and smoking flax He will not quench." Reeds bend in the breeze beautifully, but if you bump one hard enough, it creases and bends over. God says that if you are spiritually or physically frail or wounded, He won't allow you to be completely broken. Likewise, if you are a smoking flax, He'll see to it that you aren't quenched.

A smoking flax is like the glowing ember at the tip of a candle wick—like that on a backyard tiki torch. Depending on the type of fuel used, when you blow out the flame, momentarily it looks like it's out, but it's not—half a second later, it comes back to life. How is it possible? That little ember.

If your faith is but a little glowing ember, it can be reignited by the Holy Spirit's work in you. But once you're ignited, are you okay with God using you in the way He desires? "Oh yes, Lord, I will follow You anywhere," you say. Good, but better yet, say, "Lord, I will follow You anywhere, and please give me the grace and ability to do so." Because what if the doctor sends you for X-rays and the radiologist finds a lump? What happens when you leave your job on Friday and come back on Monday morning only to see someone else's car in your reserved spot and find out your key no longer works in the front door? In situations like those, God is offering you the chance to speak to a nurse or a job recruiter about Jesus. He is calling you to communicate the gospel to someone who would never listen to a podcast or attend a crusade, let alone a church service.

When we talk about knowing the gospel, are you aware of the responsibility that you and I have? If you know the gospel, and I am presuming that you do, you are supposed to share it. Romans 10:15 says, "How beautiful are the feet of those who preach the gospel of peace." For the world to meet Jesus, you must take Him beyond your church's walls to the construction site, the sales office, and the factory floor.

This may sound strange to some, but it's time for you and me to hear with our spirit. Romans 10:17 says, "Faith comes by hearing, and hearing by the word of God." Many Christians use that verse in connection with evangelism, but it also communicates an incredible personal challenge. The phrase "the word of God" may make us think of the Greek word *logos*, which, in John 1:1-4, refers to Jesus Christ, the Son of God. But in Romans 10:17, "word" is altogether different. It is the Greek word *rhema*, which means a saying or speech. This is vitally important to both how and when we express our faith.

Rhema is the issuing of a charge, the giving of a discourse. It is the Word of God for the "now." It is God's specific word for a specific time, but the key is knowing the *logos*—the speech or thought of God from the Scriptures. God has committed the word of reconciliation to us so that we might plead with people to turn to Christ for salvation. We need to stop tiptoeing around. When the Holy Spirit prompts us to tell someone about the glories of heaven and horrors of hell, and that salvation is in Christ alone, we cannot wait. That person needs to hear the Word of God now! "We then, as workers together with Him also plead with you not to receive the grace of God in vain. For He says: 'In an acceptable time I have heard you, and in the day of salvation I have helped you.' Behold, now is the accepted time; behold, now is the day of salvation" (2 Corinthians 6:1-2).

HEAVEN'S DEVOTION

Today, as I write, it's as if five pounds of geopolitical tension has been stuffed into a three-pound container and is threatening to explode. Recent events in the Middle East have set the globe on edge once again. Key regional players have been upended, allowing others to rear their ugly heads. And then there is America. In a show of support and military might, the US deployed tremendous naval firepower into the region.

Previously, I took a measure of comfort in our country's military strength. That is no longer true. America could very well be sailing to her demise. Couldn't happen? Watch out, believer. God says never trust in your chariots (Psalm 20:7), and I want to add, especially when they have the potential to become entangled with the countries prophetically mentioned in Ezekiel 38:2-6. If America is somehow taken out of the picture, Israel will be alone, abandoned by the nations of the world, just as Bible prophecy says will happen.

Why do I mention events that could very well be a reality before this book lands in your hands? Because they are catapulting us closer to the day when Jesus will come for His church, proving (as if we needed more proof!) that idleness is not an option. By the work of God and His goodness, heaven is where we will be one day. But if you and I truly have faith, we will be serious about our faith right now and absolutely devoted to acting in accordance with God's very nature, purpose, and will.

If you do not have a firm grasp on the fullness of God's grace, this may sound legalistic, but there is no reason for a sloppy Christian life. God has done everything needed to bring us into heaven, and He will stay beside us until we arrive. Yet we have no excuse for being haphazard in our devotion to Him who has loved us with an everlasting love. I agree with New Testament theologian Simon Kistemaker: "If believers are to be looking forward to living eternally in a home of righteousness on the new Earth, then now on this Earth ought they to be practicing righteousness."[2]

I believe God's Spirit is saying to the church, "Practice living kingdom life here and now so that when God's kingdom comes, it isn't going to be much different for you." Yes, you and I live in a fallen world. Yes, you and I will be tripped up by sin from time to time. None of us are perfect or sinless, but that's why grace and repentance are there to get you back on course. But act kingdom-like now. Second Peter 3:18 says, "Grow in the grace and knowledge of our Lord and Savior Jesus Christ. To Him be the glory both now and forever. Amen."

Great theologians have two opinions about what verse 18 means and persuade us to pick one or the other. I pick both. Here is why: One group says, "Start living out kingdom life until Jesus shows up." I have no problem with that. The other group says, "You don't have to do it. It's the Holy Spirit in you. He'll do kingdom life in you and through you until He shows up." I agree with that statement as well. I believe both theological camps are right. The Holy Spirit in you is the kingdom of God—that's what He represents.

When the Holy Spirit is at work in you, He helps you do things that please God because pleasing God is the outflow of the Spirit's work in you, bringing you to completion in Christ. In these last days, our desire should be to grow at a pace that outstrips that of evil.

Throughout the Scriptures, I see God exercising extreme patience with His people Israel. He waits for them to repent of their wayward coldness toward Him before executing judgment. God waits for them to pick up the Scriptures, believe them, apply them to their lives, and be useful for His kingdom. And today, I see God exercising the same longsuffering and patience with the church as He did with Israel. He is waiting, but what will those who are in the church decide to do? And before you turn the page, I encourage you to make that question personal. Ask the Lord, "How can I fulfill Your command to occupy until You come?"

When the Holy Spirit is at work in you, He helps you do things that please God because pleasing God is the outflow of the Spirit's work in you, bringing you to completion in Christ.

Years ago, my wife and I visited a castle where English general Lord Oliver Cromwell was said to have stayed, on occasion, when passing through the area. Perhaps you've heard or read about Lord Cromwell's leadership and military exploits, but a well-known quote attributed to him applies to every Christian's life here and now.

During Cromwell's time as the Lord Protector of the British Isles, there was a shortage of silver for minting coins. He directed his men to see what they could do to find the needed metal. They reported back that there was none to be found except in the churches. They said, "The statues are made of metal. The saints are made of metal, some gold and some silver. Outside of that, there is none." Lord Cromwell replied, "Get back to the churches, melt down the saints, and get them into circulation!" Isn't that great? I love it.

Cromwell's directive is custom-made for the remarkable times in which we live. May God take us out of our comfort zones, melt us down, and put us into circulation to fight the good fight of faith until He receives us into glory!

CHAPTER 14

BEFORE I LET YOU GO

If you're anything like me, I imagine you enjoy visiting museums like the Smithsonian's National Museum of Natural History. Institutions like this have a tangible quality that allows us to step back in time. However, one of the difficult challenges facing a museum curator is making presentations or exhibits move out of the past and into our present day. Anyone who has ever put together a class project, commemorative display, or any kind of reenactment knows this is no small feat.

I bring this up because when it comes to the practical outworking of the Holy Spirit, believers often experience the same difficulty. Far too many Christians relegate the Holy Spirit's work to the saints of old and fail to appropriate Jesus' promise, "You shall receive power when the Holy Spirit has come upon you, and you shall be witnesses to Me" (Acts 1:8), for themselves.

So, before I let you go, it is essential to look at the Holy Spirit's association with the Christian's bold faith because such faith is impossible without Him. We cannot and will not survive without a fresh infusion of the power, the purpose, and the Person of God, the Holy Spirit. Believer, the same exceedingly great power that raised Christ from the dead is at work in you! (Ephesians 1:19-20).

THE HOLY SPIRIT IN HISTORY

When we look back at the distant past, through the lens of Scripture, we see from the beginning of the creation of the material elements of the physical universe that the ever-present third Person of the divine Trinity, the Holy Spirit, was there. "The earth was without form, and void; and darkness was on the face of the deep. And the Spirit of God was hovering over the face of the waters" (Genesis 1:2).

Moving forward, Scripture also reveals that the Holy Spirit was the One who came upon God's servants selected to do His will on the earth—as with the patriarch Abraham. The Spirit of God spoke to him, arousing his curiosity to such a degree that Abraham's lifelong inclination toward his culture's pagan idols and their system of worship immediately proved inadequate. And the Spirit of God beckoned Abraham out of Ur of the Chaldees.

When God summoned specific men and women to become the judges over the people of Israel, the hallmark of their careers was marked by the power of His Holy Spirit. From the incredible feats and wisdom of Israel's judge, Deborah, to Samson's sad and sorry witness but ultimate triumph, the Holy Spirit was there at work.

Look further in Scripture, and we read of the Holy Spirit at work in the life of Samuel. Dedicated to God and led by His Spirit from his tenderest years, Samuel grew into the man who would become Israel's kingmaker and chief among the many prophets of Israel. Looking further, we see the Holy Spirit working in various battles between Israel and its surrounding neighbors. It was the Holy Spirit who caused confusion to fall upon the ranks of the wicked to bring about incredible supernatural feats of military prowess through a handful of God's chosen people (1 Samuel 14:20).

Space does not allow us to recount all the tremendous exploits God did through His people. The author of Hebrews put it like this:

What more shall I say? For the time would fail me to tell of Gideon and Barak and Samson and Jephthah, also of David and Samuel and the prophets: who through faith subdued kingdoms, worked righteousness, obtained promises, stopped the mouths of lions, quenched the violence of fire, escaped the edge of the sword, out of weakness were made strong, became valiant in battle, turned to flight the armies of the aliens. Women received their dead raised to life again. Others were tortured, not accepting deliverance, that they might obtain a better resurrection. Still others had trial of mockings and scourgings, yes, and of chains and imprisonment. They were stoned, they were sawn in two, were tempted, were slain with the sword. They wandered about in sheepskins and goatskins, being destitute, afflicted, tormented—of whom the world was not worthy (Hebrews 11:32-38).

Likewise, church history is filled with accounts of believers who refused to bow their knee to anything or anyone other than the Lord Jesus Christ—famous among them are Nicholas Ridley and Hugh Latimer. They believed that all people are equal before the cross, God's Word should be taught freely and obeyed without regard to the traditions of men, and that God could be approached simply and directly without an earthly mediator. For their scriptural views, they were arrested, tried, and burned at the stake, in Oxford, England. As flames rose around them, witnesses recorded that Latimer encouraged Ridley, "Be of good comfort Master Ridley, and play the man. We shall this day light such a candle, by God's grace in England, as I trust shall never be put out."[1]

Ridley and Latimer knew the God whom they believed and what they were in Christ. They were convinced that biblical truth can be lived out practically with divine force and great effect, and they were right. Their bold witness, along with others, ultimately transformed the church.

I am also reminded of the remarkable history of America's two Great Awakenings brought about by the moving of the Spirit of God. How did the First Great Awakening come about? It was the result of yielded men of God and profound preachers and teachers of His Word who lit a fledgling nation ablaze to become one nation under God and to establish the Bible as its chief book of education.

How did our Founding Fathers pursue such a glorious and, if I might say, impossible pursuit? They turned back to ancient times to see what God did in the Scriptures. They studied the Hebrew Old Testament and the Greek New Testament accounts. And because God moved in times past, they had the boldness to seek Him in their present circumstances, hoping and trusting that He might want to move again. A new nation was birthed, and with it, history was made.

Like the First Great Awakening, all who lived during the Second Great Awakening and were eyewitnesses attested that it occurred by a mighty outpouring of the Holy Spirit stirring the hearts of God's people. Today, the United States owes its existence, pleasant attributes, and all things good to nothing less than a divine work of the Holy Spirit.

THE HOLY SPIRIT IS KNOWABLE

Many people unfamiliar with the Holy Spirit or fearful of Him suppose that He is impossible to know—quite the contrary. Throughout the Bible, Scripture reveals the marvelous characteristics of God's Spirit. The psalmist knew and revered the Holy Spirit as evidenced in Psalm 51:11-12. He is intelligent (1 Corinthians 2:10-11). He has feelings, emotions, and can be grieved (Ephesians 4:30), and His will is always in accordance with God the Father's (1 Corinthians

12:11). The Holy Spirit speaks (John 15:26), and when He does, He will never contradict the Word of God because it is the Spirit who is the author of the Scriptures (2 Peter 1:21).

To the wicked, Genesis 6:3 reveals the Spirit as a restrainer who will not always put up with evil: "The LORD said, 'My Spirit shall not strive with man forever.'" But to believers, the Holy Spirit is our teacher and, as such, will reveal to us the meaning and application of Scripture to our lives (John 14:26). And He becomes our guide through our Christian experience (Romans 8:14). One of the aspects of the Spirit's nature that I find most comforting is that He speaks to the Father and the Son on our behalf (verse 26).

We also understand from Acts 10:19-21 that the Holy Spirit is to be obeyed. And as the third Person of the Godhead, the Spirit can be lied to, which carries a profound warning to all. The apostle Peter confronted Ananias and Sapphira about their conspiracy to make themselves look more spiritual by lying about the details of the sale of a piece of their property. Scripture says that in this case, they sinned against the Holy Spirit and, indeed, against God (Acts 5:3-4).

All of what you have just read is because the Holy Spirit possesses *all* the divine characteristics of God the Father and God the Son. He is omniscient or all-knowing (1 Corinthians 2:10-11). He is always omnipresent or present everywhere at the same time (Psalm 139:7) and is omnipotent or all-powerful (Genesis 1:2). In 1 John 5:6, we read that He is truth, and because God is holy (Isaiah 6:3), and the Holy Spirit is the third Person of the Godhead, we know the Holy Spirit is holy. Romans 8:2 tells us that He is life, and in Isaiah 40:13, the Spirit's characteristic is wisdom.

We've seen that the Holy Spirit is a person with personality, which means that although He is spirit and not physical, nor human, He can be blasphemed against. Jesus said this of Him in Matthew 12:31: "I say to you, every sin and blasphemy will be forgiven men, but the blasphemy against the Spirit will not be forgiven men." If that is not a warning, I don't know what is. But perhaps one of the most serious and grave warnings is that the Holy Spirit can be resisted: "You stiff-necked and uncircumcised in heart and ears! You always resist the Holy Spirit; as your fathers did, so do you" (Acts 7:51).

I believe that resistance to the Holy Spirit explains the insanity of today's world. Why is our culture so violent, mean, and ugly? It is because of those who, in these last days filled with deception, have chosen to resist the Holy Spirit's words of warning and challenges to their sin and evil conduct. "This is the condemnation, that the light has come into the world, and men loved darkness rather than light, because their deeds were evil. For everyone practicing evil hates the light and does not come to the light, lest his deeds should be exposed" (John 3:19-20). What a profound and accurate diagnosis of our human condition outside of Christ.

THE HOLY SPIRIT'S EMPOWERMENT

The church is to be the bastion of all truth and a clarion voice of hope in a hopeless world. Then why is the twenty-first-century Western church so anemic and frail, even saltless and lightless? It is because the church has largely sought to be the church without the power of the Holy Spirit.

We have surrendered our hot pursuit of God for stagnation. We have been taught to swallow more of a storybook-type allegorical view of Scripture rather than the living, breathing, double-edged sword of God's burning Word (Hebrews 4:12). We have left off personal intimacy with the Holy Spirit. Yet, should He not be in possession of us? Is not the Bible shouting at us that God wants to do the unimaginable through His children? Through you? We must get back to Him, who is our source of power to do the impossible if we are going to make a difference.

Our dilemma is when we pick up the Bible, we can find ourselves being the problem. We see God wanting to do more than what we read in the book of Acts. Why is that? Because we live in a darker, more sinister age that is much closer to the end.

God wants to take His Word and use it in believers who are yielded and surrendered so as to experience a life filled with His dynamic—the explosive power of the Holy Spirit. The same power was experienced in the upper room when the Holy Spirit came upon the believers who were there (Acts 2:1-4). They were filled with power and were sent out into the world. They exercised diversities of gifts by the same Spirit. They reached their world for Christ as they decreased and He increased. They spoke, and Jesus was proclaimed, and the world shook when His followers advanced from town to town, city to city, and continent to continent.

Daniel 11:32 says, "The people who know their God shall be strong, and carry out great exploits." Yes, this passage refers to those during the tribulation period, but God is no respecter of persons. The same Holy Spirit who was present in the upper room will be present then and is the same Holy Spirit present with us today.

We must remember the Holy Spirit's vital role in personal and private worship. Whether it's Sunday morning or a midweek service, privately or in a small group, we should possess a sense of reverential awe and expectancy when we come together to enter the presence of the Lord. But how is that achieved? You can experience it by being aware of the Holy Spirit's presence as you approach God. Know that it is the Spirit who is leading you into what I like to think of as a moment of discovery. You are coming to experience God's will in your worship, and in so doing, you fully anticipate God speaking direction, wisdom, and guidance.

Please allow me to exhort you: May I press upon you the great need for you to practice a disciplined Christian life and get alone with God? Expect Him to speak specific things that are personal to you from His Word.

I say to you, ask, and it will be given to you; seek, and you will find; knock, and it will be opened to you. For everyone who asks receives, and he who seeks finds, and to him who knocks it will be opened. If a son asks for bread from any father among you, will he give him a stone? Or if he asks for a fish, will he give him a serpent instead of a fish? Or if he asks for an egg, will he offer him a scorpion? If you then, being evil, know how to give good gifts to your children, how much more will your heavenly Father give the Holy Spirit to those who ask Him! (Luke 11:9-13).

And finally, the Bible also makes it wonderfully known that the Holy Spirit calls us into ministry (Acts 13:4). He is the great commissioner of the work of God on the earth and calls His people to certain tasks (Act 8:29).

THE HOLY SPIRIT PUTS FAITH TO WORK

There has been a consistent thread from the very beginning of this book to where we are right now. God's people have always operated in the realm of faith in a way that would not allow their faith to remain theoretical. Faith becomes practical, usable, and enduring when faith in Jesus Christ is brought together with God's Word and the power of the Holy Spirit in conjunction with the will of the Father.

As a pastor, I have watched God take everyday people from all walks of life and use them to transform the world around them, precisely as Hebrews chapter 11 says will happen. I have included a few real-life experiences to encourage you to stand boldly for Christ wherever He sends you.

Academics: A tenured public-school teacher was recognized by her colleagues as having a bright future because of her excellence in the classroom. But when woke ideology overtook her school district, they required her to promote and cooperate with LBGTQ demands regarding her students. She quickly informed her administration that she could not comply because it violated her faith and personal convictions. In response, she was pressured, bullied, and finally fired. She lost her career for taking a stand but would not allow it to go unchallenged. We met and prayed and sought the Lord as to what should be done. I love that God's Word always rises to the occasion, and 2 Corinthians 10:6 became her guide: "And being ready to punish all disobedience when your obedience is fulfilled."

She determined to take a stand. She would not waver nor comply. She would not give in to the demands of evil. Rather, she exposed them by her obedience to Christ and punished disobedience by filing a lawsuit against her school district. That battle continues, but she has become an inspiration to teachers across the United States.

Law: A young lady from our church excelled academically, and because she had a strong biblical foundation, when she studied American history, God's role in our nation became abundantly clear to her. From there she felt compelled to pursue a law degree. Upon passing the bar exam, she became a United States federal attorney working for the Department of Justice before moving to a law firm specializing in constitutional freedom. She now defends and argues the cases of Christians who have been wrongfully treated or had their constitutional rights abused.

Armed forces: A young man from our congregation took his biblical worldview into the United States Air Force, where the quality of his character and abilities made him stand out among his fellow soldiers. God promoted him, as He often does regarding those who obey Him. The man excelled above others and, at a young age, was given the command of several key satellites responsible for US national defense and security and several other notable countries. Eventually, he was promoted to positions leading to the US Space Force before leaving the military. This man continues to stand boldly for faith and freedom as he uses his skills to defend and uphold the truth.

Athletics: A well-known woman won three Olympic gold medals and two World Championships in her sport. Knowing that it was God who gifted her with unique abilities, she took the platform He provided and used it to witness to others God's love. And even now, at the time of this writing, she has an active speaking schedule encouraging athletes around the world to pursue not only their athletic passion, but to do it for the glory of God.

Politics: Most people talk about a problem in their community, but one concerned mother decided to do something about it. Through the teaching of God's Word, the Holy Spirit prompted her to engage the culture and run for office in a local election. With no prior experience, she was an unlikely candidate, but God had a plan. She won and is now known as a fierce defender of conservative values in her community. And although she is the recipient of false accusations and death threats for her refusal to entertain ungodly agendas, she continues to serve with diligence and passion.

I also want to highlight the healthcare professionals, first responders, and airline pilots who suffered public ridicule, ostracizing, furloughs, demotions, and job losses because they refused the controversial COVID-19 vaccine. Why did these believers decide to hold fast to their convictions? Was it based on feelings, or a rebellious streak? Were they just looking for a fight? The answer is no. I know them and their stories, and I know their witness and love for Christ. These men and women boldly stood their ground and were later vindicated as right in their refusal.

And countless others who stand firm in faith day in and day out, week after week, year after year, are known only to God. Without apology, they boldly stand unwavering and steadfast, believing that God has proven Himself faithful in their lives and will never abandon them. I believe that this also describes a great assembly of believers who span the globe at this very moment. God has placed His people from San Diego to Santiago, from Hong Kong to Honduras, on every continent and in every city, hamlet, and village, and they are standing firm on the truth of God.

THE HOLY SPIRIT COMMISSIONS

And so, as you've come to the end of this book, I would like to believe, to imagine, that you and I together have come to this moment of commissioning. *Commissioning* is a word often used in Christian circles regarding ministry, evangelism, or some other spiritual endeavor, and rightly so. It is, as we have spoken of, the job of the Holy Spirit to commission believers into a life of ministry. But this wasn't reserved only for the believer. Jesus Christ received a commission from His Father as He waged a spiritual battle in prayer in the Garden of Gethsemane.

I have often visited that garden, which still stands today just east of the Temple Mount in Jerusalem. Some of the ancient olive trees are recorded to be the offspring of those who stood watch that night as Jesus struggled with His Father, asking if there was another way of salvation (see Matthew 26:39). If you remember, Jesus, in His humanity and physical weakness, cried out in prayer, "Father, if there is any other way, let this cup be removed from Me." The answer arrived from heaven—a tear-shaped answer for which we will be eternally grateful—"There is no other way for mankind to be saved."

There was no other answer. There was no other plan. This was the plan. This was Jesus' calling—the commission placed upon the Messiah before time began. After praying, Jesus would arise and arouse His disciples to meet His betrayers en route to the willful sacrifice of Himself. Jesus' sacrifice is matchless.

Jesus' last recorded words to His apostles in Matthew 28:19-20 was His commissioning to the work He set before them. It is from these verses, known as the Great Commission, that all Christ-followers have their orders. Untold numbers of men and women have heeded and obeyed Jesus' command, but one very special young man comes to mind.

Born in Long Beach, California, on April 5, 1981, Michael Anthony Monsoor would eventually become a typical US Navy SEAL—if such a thing is possible. I say that because there is nothing typical about SEAL training, duties, achievements, nor persona.

Michael Mansoor was devoted to not only the preservation and safety and freedom of his nation, but he was also committed to the liberation and freedom of the Iraqi people. He, like others, hoped they might someday have the ability and the right to make their own decisions and choices. And yet, in his commissioning, little did he know the cost of his call.

It happened on September 29, 2006, in the Iraqi village of Ramadi—a well-documented day that would later make news headlines. The US Navy SEALs were embedded with Iraqi army members because of frequent and ongoing insurgent gun battles waged for the control of the village. That day, Michael Anthony Mansoor offered the ultimate sacrifice.

Monsoor and several others were atop a roof when an insurgent combatant threw a grenade. It hit Monsoor squarely in the chest and fell at his feet. Positioned next to the only exit, Michael could have escaped injury. In fact, he was the only one who could have done so. Instead, Michael immediately threw himself on the grenade, cradling it in a fetal position as he was trained. Seconds later, the grenade detonated. Michael absorbed the force of the blast that would have killed his fellow military brothers, including members of the Iraqi army. He was immediately medivacked out of the area but died of his wounds within 30 minutes.

On the day Michael Monsoor was laid to rest in San Diego's Fort Rosecrans National Cemetery, an incredible scene took place as his fellow SEALs gathered to say farewell to their brother. Before the coffin was moved from the hearse, those men formed columns on both sides of the pallbearer's route. As the coffin was carried to the gravesite, one SEAL was inspired to tear from his uniform his gold trident pin—the unmistakable symbol of a US Navy SEAL. He drove it into the top of the simple wooden coffin with the strike of his fist as though the action was a choreographed protocol. Following his lead, one brother after another took their trident pin—that spectacular, beautiful emblem—and did the same.

The plain coffin lid was transformed by the shining gold of each SEAL's trident pin—imbuing Monsoor's coffin with their own identity and honors—representing the only sacrifice his brothers could make for him. Michael Monsoor's body was laid to rest until the Day of Resurrection.

I find it fascinating that Monsoor gave his life that others might have a choice with theirs. I find it humbling that he instantly threw himself upon certain death that others might live. And I find it remarkable that a man who had achieved the epitome of status as a US Navy SEAL willingly ended his earthly career that others might live on to enjoy theirs. Can you see the correlation, in some small way, to what Jesus Christ has done for us? Perhaps in this, you can see a picture of the great sacrifice that God—who dwelt in eternity yet veiled Himself in human flesh and made atonement so you and I might live.

The influence and commitment of Michael Anthony Monsoor lives on in a practical way. When you leave downtown San Diego via the Coronado Bay Bridge, you may catch a glimpse of the USS Michael Monsoor (DDG-1001). If it is in port, it's impossible to miss. Commissioned on January 26, 2019, the Zumwalt-class guided-missile destroyer is one of the world's most advanced surface warfare ships designed to protect and preserve global freedom. Believer, that ship, like its namesake, was commissioned to do a job, and so are you.

As noble and worthy as any commissioning is, it begins with the determination to decide and exercise choice. And as we have learned, one single choice made in a split second can have eternal consequences. The choices that you and I make set in motion the kind of life we will live. Will it be a transformed life of faith, or something less? By choosing to exercise biblical faith, your life will not be stationary nor static. It's impossible. Why? Because as children of the living God, we are in this world to spread His love, grace, and message.

When you walk upright before God and make decisions based on His Word, you will live a defiant, faith-filled life empowered by the Holy Spirit. You will take a bold stand.

Choices and decisions must be made. What will we do with the opportunities we are given? I suggest choosing a defiant life. Defiant in the face of evil. So, when the world says sin, you don't. When the world says bow, you stand. "The LORD is on my side; I will not fear. What can man do to me?" (Psalm 118:6). When you walk upright before God and make decisions based on His Word, you will live a defiant, faith-filled life empowered by the Holy Spirit. You will take a bold stand.

COMMISSIONED FOR RIGHTEOUSNESS'S SAKE

Jesus Christ commissioned believers to go into all the world, preach the gospel, and make disciples of all people, baptizing them in the name of the Father, the Son, and the Holy Spirit. We are to take to this world all that is right, all that is good, and all that is the gospel, for righteousness's sake. And with that, we are to be, in some way, protecting, learning, growing, and developing with our fellow warriors, every single day.

The day might come when you or I are hit by a grenade to the chest, so to speak, and be given, in that split-second moment, the instant commissioning of laying down our lives. That may or may not come to us in this life, but as I look around the world and see the growing hostility toward Christianity, persecution could very well visit us in the West, as in other parts of the globe. After all, why would any part of the modern church be exempt from the nearly perpetual physical violence and persecution levied against believers throughout these last 2,000 years? But be of good cheer. With Jesus' commission comes a glorious promise: "I am with you always, even to the end of the age" (Matthew 28:20). The fact that Jesus Christ is always with you and me is proof positive of the Holy Spirit's enduring presence as well.

Though you and I may be simple beings—our very flesh and bone and blood are comprised of the basic elements of this earth—we are living, breathing testimonies to God's creative power. Within us is housed a treasure that no value can be placed upon—no wealth or gold could provide nor match what the Bible tells us: "We have this treasure in earthen vessels, that the excellence of the power may be of God and not of us" (2 Corinthians 4:7). Each of us can exercise a bold faith because of the Spirit's power residing within us and upon us. He can and will lead us into the most wonderful, glorious, and worthy battles for truth.

Today, it is up to you to decide: *Am I willing to stand boldly with Jesus Christ and the leading of the Holy Spirit to draw me into what He has for me—the great commissioning for my life as a believer?*

For many, the full extent of your commission is yet to be revealed. But as you seek God, and He shows it to you in His Word, there will be a focus and a release of the Spirit's power as you yield and commit yourself to His plans. You will live a life of meaning, purpose, and holy sacrifice, just as the apostle Paul wrote to the believers in Rome:

I urge you, brothers and sisters, in view of God's mercy, to offer your bodies as a living sacrifice, holy and pleasing to God—this is your true and proper worship. Do not conform to the pattern of this world, but be transformed by the renewing of your mind. Then you will be able to test and approve what God's will is—His good, pleasing and perfect will (Romans 12:1-2 NIV).

You are now, at this moment, at this time, being commissioned, not by me, nor some sergeant, commander, or general, but by your Shepherd, the Shepherd King. The Lord Jesus Christ is calling you, as the instruments of hope in this world, to exercise a biblically based bold faith.

May we live daily for Christ by His power and for His glory as never before. And from this time forward—until we finish our race, or the Lord appears and calls us upward—may our faith stand the test of time, stamped with the pure gold of a life defined and refined by sacrifice and service.

I pray that God has stirred your heart with the realization that He has placed you where you're standing to be a witness for Him—equal to all who have gone before. Now, go forth into a world that needs Jesus.

In the footsteps of Jesus Christ Himself and to His glory alone, unto God be all praise.

Awaiting His return,
Jack Hibbs

*See, I have set before you an open door,
and no one can shut it; for you have a little strength,
have kept My word, and have not denied My name.*

REVELATION 3:8

INDEX OF SCRIPTURE REFERENCES

CHAPTER 1

Exodus 21:1-6
Psalm 90:12
Proverbs 28:1
Matthew 4:18-20; 7:21-23; 14:29; 26:74
John 1:12; 3:3-8; 8:34-36
Acts 1:4-5; 2:1-4; 13:22
Romans 1:1; 7:17; 15:2-3; 6:16, 19

1 Corinthians 6:19
2 Corinthians 3:18; 5:17
Galatians 2:20
Ephesians 4:30
Philippians 2:5-7
Colossians 1:15-21; 3:3
1 Timothy 1:15
2 Peter 1:1

CHAPTER 2

Psalms 22:5; 25:1-3; 37:3-4; 138:8; 139:16-18
Jeremiah 1:5
John 14:8-9, 23; 17:3
Romans 8:1, 15-16; 10:11
2 Corinthians 2:15-16; 3:5; 5:10; 12:9
Galatians 5:22-23

Ephesians 1:4, 5; 2:10; 3:20
Philippians 2:13
Colossians 2:10
2 Timothy 3:16-17
Hebrews 4:16
2 Peter 1:2-5
Revelation 3:5; 20:11-15

CHAPTER 3

Exodus 4:11
2 Samuel 11:1-27

Psalm 51
Jeremiah 1:6, 7-8

Matthew 25:14-30
Mark 12:31
John 6:68; 7:37-39; 8:28-29;
    15:5, 7-8
Romans 5:9; 12:1-2
1 Corinthians 1:18; 13; 15:52
2 Corinthians 5:14; 10:12
Galatians 5:6

Ephesians 2:8; 5:1
1 Thessalonians 4:3
2 Timothy 1:7
Hebrews 6:1-2
James 4:8
2 Peter 1:5-8
1 John 4:9-11, 16

CHAPTER 4

Psalm 90:12
Isaiah 26:3; 40:8
Jeremiah 3:15
Matthew 12:34; 24:11
Luke 15:18
John 3:3; 14:6; 21:16-19
Acts 20:18-24; 21:13-14
1 Corinthians 3:11; 8:9
Galatians 1:6-9

Ephesians 4:29, 31-32; 5:16
Philippians 3:7
Titus 2:11-12
Hebrews 4:12; 10:38; 11
2 Peter 1:12-15
1 John 1:9
Jude 1:3, 5
Revelation 2:4-5

CHAPTER 5

1 Chronicles 12:32
Proverbs 4:25-27
Isaiah 52:7; 62:6-7
Ezekiel 3:17-21
Matthew 13:16; 16:23; 17:1-3, 5-7;
    20:21; 24:29-30; 26:56, 69-75;
    28:18
Mark 14:37, 40, 41
Luke 22:37, 63-64
John 1:14
Acts 1:1-3

1 Corinthians 15:6
2 Corinthians 13:1
Ephesians 1:19-20
Philippians 1:6
Colossians 1:15-19
2 Timothy 3:16
Hebrews 12:2; 13:20-21
2 Peter 1:16, 17, 19
1 John 1:1-2
Revelation 1:10, 17-18

CHAPTER 6

Proverbs 3:9; 11:25
Jeremiah 14:14; 20:9
Amos 7:7
Luke 14:31
John 14:6
Acts 4:12; 20:28-29
Romans 1:20; 3:23
1 Corinthians 6:9
2 Corinthians 9:6-7
Galatians 3:24-25; 5:9

Colossians 1:5-6
1 Thessalonians 5:21
1 Timothy 4:1-2
2 Timothy 2:3-4; 4:2-3
Hebrews 1:1
2 Peter 2:1-3
1 John 2:19; 4:2-3
Jude 1:12
Revelation 21:8

CHAPTER 7

Numbers 22–24; 22:22-32; 32:23
Psalm 7:11
Proverbs 6:27
Matthew 7:13-15
Romans 2:15; 3:10-18; 6:13; 13:1
1 Corinthians 6:20
Galatians 2:20
Philippians 4:8

Colossians 3:1-2
1 Timothy 6:6, 10, 12
Hebrews 4:1-2, 12; 6:4-6
1 Peter 1:13; 4:17
2 Peter 1:2-3; 2; 2:10-16
Jude 1:9, 21
Revelation 2:5, 14

CHAPTER 8

Genesis 3:15; 6; 6:1-4, 9-10; 19:1
Exodus 22:19
Job 1:6; 2:1; 38:4, 7
Isaiah 14:9, 12-14
Ezekiel 28:13-15
Daniel 4:13; 10:12-13
Matthew 12:43; 24:37
Luke 1:35; 4:1-13; 15:10
John 10:27-30
Romans 1:26-27; 8:35, 38-39; 11:25
1 Corinthians 12:2; 14:38

2 Corinthians 1:8; 2:11; 10:3-6; 15:16
Ephesians 1:13-14
Colossians 1:16; 2:15
1 Thessalonians 4:13
2 Timothy 3:1
Hebrews 13:2
James 4:7
1 Peter 5:8-9
2 Peter 2:4, 9
Jude 1:6-7
Revelation 12:4, 9; 20:7-15

CHAPTER 9

Genesis 6:9; 19:1-15, 24-25
Isaiah 6:1-8; 66:15-16
Joel 2:11
Matthew 10:16
Luke 7:47; 9:62
John 14:21-23; 15:11
Acts 20:24

Romans 7:15
2 Corinthians 5:17; 10:4-6
Ephesian 5:8
Colossians 2:14
1 Timothy 6:17
2 Peter 2:5-8; 3:9
1 John 2:15

CHAPTER 10

Exodus 32:8-10, 15-18
Jeremiah 31:31-33
Matthew 5:28; 23:3-4
Luke 12:1
John 3:3; 10:9-10; 14:17
Romans 8:28
1 Corinthians 6:9-10

2 Corinthians 1:8-9; 11:13-15
Galatians 2:16; 5:1
Philippians 3:12-14
2 Timothy 3:16
2 Peter 2:17, 19, 20
Jude 1:12
Revelation 3:2, 8

CHAPTER 11

Genesis 5:24
2 Kings 2:11
Isaiah 26:19-21
Jeremiah 30:7
Zechariah 2:8; 12:10
Matthew 24:45-49
Luke 12:35-37, 40; 19:13; 21:26, 36
John 3:16; 14:1-3; 5:24
Acts 1:9
Romans 11:26; 13:11-12
1 Corinthians 15:51-53
2 Corinthians 5:8

1 Thessalonians 1:10; 2:19; 3:13; 4:14-18; 5:6, 9
Titus 2:13
Hebrews 9:28; 10:24-25; 11:5
2 Peter 2:9; 3:4
1 John 3:2-3
Revelation 2–4; 4:1-11; 19:11-16
The chart: Matthew 24:40-41; 1 Corinthians 15:50-54; 1 Thessalonians 4:17; 5:9; 2 Thessalonians 2:4; Revelation 1:7; 3:10; 6–19; 19:14-16, 19-20

CHAPTER 12

Genesis 1:1-2, 6-7
Job 26:7; 36:27
Psalms 8:8; 14:1; 139:17-18
Isaiah 7:14; 9:6; 40:22; 42:9
Jeremiah 29:11; 31:3
Jonah 1:17
Micah 5:2
Matthew 11:28-30; 16:1-4
John 15:15

Acts 6:5, 8, 10-13; 7; 7:54-56, 60; 8:1; 17:11
Romans 1:28
1 Corinthians 2:16; 5:17
Ephesians 1:20
Philippians 3:1
Hebrews 1:2; 8:1
2 Peter 3:1-5, 16
1 John 3:1
Revelation 6:8

CHAPTER 13

Judges 4–5
Psalms 20:7; 23:4; 42:5; 121:2
Ecclesiastes 3:11
Isaiah 42:3
Ezekiel 38:2-6
Matthew 6:25-33; 14:30-31
John 1:1-4

Romans 8:24-25, 26, 28-30; 10:15, 17
2 Corinthians 6:1-2
Ephesians 1:3-4
Philippians 2:12-13
Hebrews 6:1
2 Peter 1:10; 2:11; 3:18

CHAPTER 14

Genesis 1:2; 6:3
1 Samuel 14:20
Psalms 51:11-12; 118:6; 139:7
Isaiah 6:3; 40:13
Daniel 11:32
Matthew 12:31; 26:39; 28:19-20
Luke 11:9-13
John 3:19-20; 14:26; 15:26
Acts 1:8-9; 2:1-4; 5:3-4; 7:51; 8:29; 10:19-21; 13:4

Romans 8:2, 14, 26; 12:1-2
1 Corinthians 2:10-11; 12:11
2 Corinthians 4:7; 10:6
Ephesians 1:19-20; 4:30
Hebrews 4:12; 11; 11:32-38
2 Peter 1:21
1 John 5:6
Revelation 3:8

NOTES

CHAPTER 1—THE REAL YOU
1. Franklin Delano Roosevelt, "The Great Arsenal of Democracy," *American Rhetoric*, December 29, 1940, https://americanrhetoric.com/speeches/fdrarsenalofdemocracy.html.

CHAPTER 2—BELIEVE
1. "When It's Okay to Kill Your Mother," *YouTube*, https://youtu.be/LxjCdBmCCVQ?si=B-mm11bZXS4E8m_g.

CHAPTER 3—BEAR HIS IMAGE
1. A.W. Tozer, *The Knowledge of the Holy* (New York: HarperCollins, 1978), 1.
2. C.S. Lewis, *The Weight of Glory* (New York: Macmillan, 1966), 10.

CHAPTER 4—REMEMBER
1. The text on the plaque itself is all uppercase, which has been adapted here for ease of reading.
2. Warren W. Wiersbe, *On Being a Servant of God* (Nashville, TN: Thomas Nelson, 1993), 6.

CHAPTER 5—BE CONFIDENT
1. Dictionary.com, https://www.dictionary.com/browse/fact.
2. Billy Graham, "The Holy Spirit and You," *Sermons.love*, https://sermons.love/billy-graham/7860-billy-graham-the-holy-spirit-and-you.html.
3. John C. Lennox, *Can Science Explain Everything?* (Epsom, Surrey, UK: The Good Book Company, 2021), 122-123.

CHAPTER 6—WATCH AND LISTEN

1. Patrick Van Horne and Jason A. Riley, *Left of Bang* (New York: Black Irish Entertainment LLC, 2014), 15.
2. Mark Hitchcock, *The Coming Apostasy: Exposing the Sabotage of Christianity from Within* (Carol Stream, IL: Tyndale, 2017), 65.
3. Albert Barnes, *Barnes' Notes on the New Testament* (Grand Rapids, MI: Kregel, 1962), 1:448.
4. Michael Corley, "Bashir puts Bell in the hot seat," *YouTube*, April 11, 2011, https://youtu.be/6hrjcEq-l0c?si=Bvo18rohhp0j8hmd.
5. Corley, "Bashir puts Bell in the hot seat."
6. Theodoret, *Ecclesiastical History (Book V)*, Chapter 26, https://www.newadvent.org/fathers/27025.htm.
7. Ronald Reagan, "National Day of Prayer, February 2, 1984," *YouTube*, https://youtu.be/v48JPdAjGdY?si=ZtgUoxEc4ZwB6hHn.

CHAPTER 7—IN YOUR SIGHTS

1. John Adams, "Adam's Argument for the Defense: 3-4 December 1770," *Founders Online*, https://founders.archives.gov/documents/Adams/05-03-02-0001-0004-0016.
2. Warren Wiersbe, *Be Distinct* (Colorado Springs, CO: David C. Cook, 2002), 135.
3. J. Vernon McGee, *Thru the Bible, vol. V* (Pasadena, CA: Thru the Bible Radio, 1983), 738.

CHAPTER 8—IT'S DARK OUT THERE

1. Cited from Donald B. DeYoung, *Astronomy and the Bible* (Grand Rapids, MI: Baker, 2000), 127.
2. "Most American Christians Do Not Believe that Satan or the Holy Spirit Exist," *Barna*, April 13, 2009, https://www.barna.com/research/most-american-christians-do-not-believe-that-satan-or-the-holy-spirit-exist/.
3. Charles R. Swindoll, *Swindoll's Living Insights: James, 1 & 2 Peter* (Wheaton, IL: Tyndale, 2014), 326.
4. Darren Orf, "'Highly Maneuverable' UFOs Defy All Physics, Says Government Study," *Popular Mechanics*, March 13, 2023, https://www.popularmechanics.com/military/research/a43298283/ufos-defy-physics-pentagon-study/.
5. C.S. Lewis, *Mere Christianity* (Nashville, TN: Broadman & Holman, 1996), 51.

CHAPTER 9—URGENT, URGENT, URGENT!

1. This quote is widely attributed to Abraham Lincoln, but the original source is unknown.
2. Anne Helmenstine, "What Is Fulgurite? Where to Find It and How to Make It," *Science Notes*, May 16, 2023, https://sciencenotes.org/what-is-fulgurite-where-to-find-it-and-how-to-make-it/#google_vignette.
3. Andrè Von Mol, MD, "Negative Health Consequences of Same-Sex Sexual Behavior," *Christian Medical & Dental Associations*, July 27, 2011, https://cmda.org/article/negative-health-consequences-of-same-sex-sexual-behavior/.

4. Preston Sprinkle and Branson Parler, "Polyamory: Pastors' Next Sexual Frontier," *Christianity Today*, 2019, https://www.christianitytoday.com/pastors/2019/fall/polyamory-next-sexual-frontier.html.

CHAPTER 10—THE FALSE AND THE TRUE

1. Dana Mattioli, "Inside Amazon's Push to Crack Trader Joe's—and Dominate Everything," *The Wall Street Journal*, April 13, 2024, https://www.wsj.com/business/retail/amazon-the-everything-war-dana-mattioli-4966915d.
2. Lord Acton as cited at "Quote," *Online Liberty Library*, https://oll.libertyfund.org/quotes/lord-acton-writes-to-bishop-creighton-that-the-same-moral-standards-should-be-applied-to-all-men-political-and-religious-leaders-included-especially-since-power-tends-to-corrupt-and-absolute-power-corrupts-absolutely-1887.
3. "The Battle Hymn of the Republic," Julia Ward Howe, 1862.
4. Alan Redpath, *Blessings Out of Buffetings: Studies in Second Corinthians* (Santa Ana, CA: Calvary Chapel Publishing, 2007), 268.

CHAPTER 12—TODAY IS THE BEST DAY

1. Michael J. Behe, *Darwin's Black Box* (New York: Free Press, 2006), 5.
2. "Parts of the Atmosphere," *National Geographic*, https://education.nationalgeographic.org/resource/parts-atmosphere/.

CHAPTER 13—HEADING FOR HOME

1. Randy Alcorn, *Heaven* (Carol Stream, IL: Tyndale Momentum, 2004), 241.
2. Simon Kistemaker, *James, Epistles of John, Peter, and Jude* (Grand Rapids, MI: Baker, 1996), 342.

CHAPTER 14—BEFORE I LET YOU GO

1. John Foxe, *Foxe's Book of Martyrs* (Terrytown, NY: Fleming H. Revell, 1997), 309.

OTHER GREAT READING BY JACK HIBBS

A HIGH-STAKES BATTLE FOR EVERY CHRISTIAN

Jesus warned that deception would grow worse as we draw nearer to the end times, saying, "Take heed that no one deceives you" (Matthew 24:4). Distinguishing truth from error has become an increasingly challenging task—even in the church.

We live in a time when falsehoods assault us from every direction. Packaged with just enough truth to make them appear trustworthy, these counterfeits have grown more and more difficult to detect and avoid.

Living in the Daze of Deception explores the many ways error is masquerading as truth—and how you can discern the difference. From pastor Jack Hibbs, you'll learn

- the characteristics of deceivers and how they have brought harm to both secular culture and the church
- the many deceptions that are altering and replacing the truth, and how to recognize them
- the keys to standing strong as the spiritual battles surrounding us intensify

The greatest antidote to deception is truth. Equip yourself now to grow in discernment so that you can protect yourself from error and remain steadfast in your faith!

ARMING YOURSELF WITH GOD'S TRUTH IN A WORLD FULL OF LIES

Not a day goes by without falsehoods of one kind or another besieging us. Because they are often packaged with just enough truth to make them appear trustworthy, we're called to be vigilant and discerning.

In this companion workbook to *Living in the Daze of Deception*, pastor Jack Hibbs enables you to distinguish error from that which is good and right. In this informative resource, you will

- learn how to recognize different kinds of deception and how they fall short of God's truth
- explore scenarios in which deception takes place and how to best respond with wisdom, prayer, and conviction
- equip yourself with the tools God has provided for your spiritual protection and be encouraged to thrive in the face of opposition

This powerful guide will embolden you more than ever to stand strong and shine God's light into a dark world! And you'll know the confidence and peace that comes from anchoring your life in God's truth.

To learn more about Harvest House books and
to read sample chapters, visit our website:
www.HarvestHousePublishers.com

HARVEST HOUSE PUBLISHERS
EUGENE, OREGON